Contents

What you need to know about the National Tests

KEY STAGE 3 NATIONAL TESTS: HOW THEY WORK

Students between the ages of 11 and 14 (Years 7–9) cover Key Stage 3 of the National Curriculum. In May of their final year of Key Stage 3 (Year 9), all students take written National Tests (commonly known as SATs) in English, Mathematics and Science. The tests are carried out in school, under the supervision of teachers, but are marked by examiners outside the school.

The tests help to show what you have learned in these key subjects. They also help parents and teachers to know whether students are reaching the standards set out in the National Curriculum. The results may be used by your teacher to help place you in the appropriate teaching group for some of your GCSE courses.

You will probably spend around seven hours in total sitting the tests during one week in May. Most students will do two test papers in each of English, Maths and Science.

The school sends the papers away to external examiners for marking. The school will then report the results of the tests to you and your parents by the end of July, along with the results of assessments made by teachers in the classroom, based on your work throughout Key Stage 3. You will also receive a summary of the results for all students at the school, and for students nationally. This will help you to compare your performance with that of other students of the same age. The report from your school will explain to you what the results show about your progress, strengths, particular achievements and targets for development. It may also explain how to follow up the results with your teachers.

UNDERSTANDING YOUR LEVEL OF ACHIEVEMENT

The National Curriculum divides standards for performance in each subject into a number of levels, from one to eight. On average, students are expected to advance one level for every two years they are at school. By Year 9 (the end of Key Stage 3), you should be at Level 5 or 6. The table on page iii shows how you are expected to progress through the levels at ages 7, 11 and 14 (the end of Key Stages 1, 2 and 3).

For English, there are two test papers: Paper 1 assesses Reading and Writing and Paper 2 assesses your understanding of and personal response to extracts from a Shakespeare play. Paper 1 will be $1\frac{3}{4}$ hours long and Paper 2 will be $1\frac{1}{4}$ hours long. An extension paper with high level questions is also available for exceptionally able students.

More emphasis is being placed on grammar, spelling and punctuation. The Grammar section in this book will help you to achieve better marks in Papers 1 and 2. It will also help you to answer separate grammar questions.

What you need to know about the National Tests

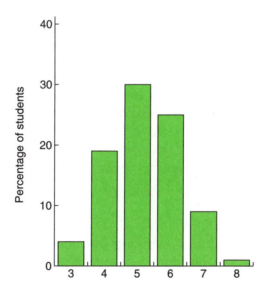

	7 years	11 years	14 years
Level 8+			☐
Level 8			▨
Level 7			▨
Level 6		☐	☐
Level 5		▨	☐
Level 4	☐	☐	▮
Level 3	▨	▮	▮
Level 2	☐	▮	▮
Level 1	▮	▮	▮

Legend:

☐ Exceptional performance

▨ Exceeded targets for age group

☐ Achieved targets for age group

▮ Working towards targets for age group

How you should progress

This book concentrates on Levels 4–7, providing two test papers with plenty of questions to practise plus an additional Grammar section. The bar chart below shows you what percentage of students nationally reached each of the levels in the 1998 tests for English.

Levels achieved in English, 1998

Preparing and practising for the English Test

ENGLISH AT KEY STAGE 3

The questions in this book will test you on the Key Stage 3 curriculum for English. For assessment purposes, the National Curriculum divides English into three sections, called Attainment Targets (ATs). The first AT, Speaking and Listening, is assessed only by the teacher in the classroom, not in the written tests. The other two ATs are Reading and Writing. The National Curriculum describes levels of performance for each of the English ATs. These AT levels are taken together to give an overall level for English. The test papers assess both Reading and Writing.

USING THIS BOOK TO HELP YOU PREPARE

This book contains four basic features:

Questions: one Reading and Writing paper and one Shakespeare paper for Levels 4–7, plus an additional Grammar section

Answers: showing you how to approach each question, and how to mark your answers using assessment criteria and model answers

Examiner's Tips: giving advice on how to improve your answers

Level Charts: showing you how to interpret your marks to arrive at a level

PAPER 1 (READING AND WRITING)

The test questions are based on the passages in the English booklet at the back of this book, which can be detached. Try Paper 1 first. Before you begin, read through the paper. Then turn to the Answers section and read through the guidance on how to approach Paper 1 in general, and how to approach each question in turn.

Carry out the test in a place where you are comfortable. You will need a pen and some lined writing paper. Read the instructions for Paper 1 carefully before you begin. Note the starting time in the box at the top of the test and time yourself during the test. When the test time is up, stop writing. If you have not finished, but wish to continue working, draw a line to show how much you completed within the test time. Then continue for as long as you wish, but do not count the 'extra' writing when you mark the paper.

Mark your answers to Paper 1 first, working through the model answers and advice. Enter your marks on the Marking Grid on page 46 and look at the Level Chart to determine your level for Paper 1.

PAPER 2 (SHAKESPEARE)

Carry out Paper 2 on a different day. Three Shakespeare extracts are reproduced in the English booklet, at the back of this book. Answer one question on the play you have studied in school. Regardless of which scenes are chosen for the actual test, you will be expected to know the entire play. This book includes scenes for each play, enabling you to practise the skills involved in answering questions about the play you know best.

Again, review how to approach Paper 2 and the question for your chosen play in the Answers section before you attempt your own answer. Answer and mark Paper 2 in the same way as Paper 1.

MARKING PAPERS 1 AND 2

When you have finished a test, turn to the section on how to mark your paper in the Answers section. Read the assessment criteria for each question, as well as the model answer, which has been marked for you. The model answers are of a very high quality and are intended to help you focus your revision. When you are judging your own answers, remember that an answer does not have to be perfect to score high marks.

It is very difficult for anyone to mark his or her own writing. When using this book, you may want to ask a parent or friend to help you judge your answers. Use the assessment criteria to award yourself the appropriate number of marks for each question. Write your score in the top half of the mark boxes on the test. Enter the marks you scored for each question on the Marking Grid on page 46. Then add them up to find the total for the test. Look at the Level Charts on page 46 to determine your level for each paper, as well as an overall level for Papers 1 and 2 combined.

GRAMMAR SECTION (SPELLING, PUNCTUATION AND GRAMMAR)

The marking schemes for Papers 1 and 2 already include consideration of your abilities to apply your knowledge of these elements of English.

However, in response to the demand for more emphasis to be placed on grammar, there is an extra section on grammar on pages 47–59. Working through this section will improve your ability in this important aspect of English. It will also help to improve your marks for Papers 1 and 2.

MARKING THE GRAMMAR SECTION

You will find the answers for this section on pages 55–59. Ask a parent, friend or teacher to help you mark your answers. Spelling is easy to mark because it is either right or wrong but the other questions may have alternative answers that are also correct. Use the Marking Grid on page 59 to find out how well you have done.

Preparing and practising for the English Test

FINALLY, AS THE TESTS DRAW NEAR

In the days before the tests, make sure you are as relaxed and confident as possible. You can help yourself by:

- ensuring you know what test papers you will be doing;

- working through practice questions, and improving your answers.

Above all, don't worry too much! Although the National Tests do matter, your achievements throughout the school year are more important and will underpin your performance in these tests. Do your best; that is all anyone can ask.

Paper 1
Reading and Writing

Instructions to student

- Carefully detach pages 1–13 from the back of this book. Fasten the pages together to make your own English booklet. Paper 1 is based on pages 1–4 of this booklet.

- First of all, you have 15 minutes to read the paper. You may make notes and annotate the passages in the booklet. Do not start to write your answers until the 15 minutes of reading time are over.

- You then have 1 hour 30 minutes to write your answers.

- Answer **all** of the questions in Sections A and B, and **one** question only from Section C.

- You should spend about:
    - 10 minutes on Question 1
    - 20 minutes on Question 2
    - 20 minutes on Question 3
    - 40 minutes on Question 4

    Your spelling and handwriting will be assessed on Section C of this paper. Check your work carefully.

This English test does not demand a particular number of words per question.

Taking this practice paper will show you how much you are able to write under timed conditions.

Look at the marks available for each question. This is shown in the box in the margin, for example,

15

In the 15 minutes of reading time, you should first skim read in order to get a sense of the whole paper. Then read the passages, questions and assignments more carefully.

Remember, effective reading and writing is dependent on **thinking** and (within the limits of a test situation) **planning**.

1

Paper 1

Section A

Read the passage **Talking in Whispers** *which is on pages 1–2 of the English booklet.*

Then answer Question 1 and Question 2.

1   The first 61 lines describe what Andres sees and does.

> **Give your impressions of what is happening and how Andres is involved.**

In your answer you should comment on:
- what is happening to the prisoners;
- what Andres does;
- what Andres thinks and feels.

You should support your ideas with words and phrases from the passage.

2   Read the rest of the passage from line 62 to the end. The soldiers become more violent and this is described in more detail. You may also notice, however, that Andres now has the means to reduce or even stop any more violence in the future.

> **Show how Andres is affected by the increasing danger and explain why there is a chance of doing something about stopping this violence in the future.**

In your answer you should comment on:
- how the writer uses these details;
- the American photographer, his role and importance;
- the behaviour of the soldiers;
- Andres' reactions.

You should support your ideas with words and phrases from the passage.

6

Q1

11

Q2

Section B

Read the Amnesty International pamphlet reproduced on pages 3–4 of the English booklet.

Amnesty International sends leaflets like this to young people, asking them to become involved.

Now answer Question 3.

3

> **The leaflet is designed to persuade young people to join Amnesty International. Point out how it does so.**

In your answer you should comment on:

- how the writer has selected information about Amnesty;

- the way words, layout and images are used in the leaflet to persuade you;

- whether you think the leaflet succeeds.

Paper 1

Section C

Choose **ONE** *of the following:*

4 EITHER

a

> **Write about a threatening situation. You could write about a real or an imaginary event. Try to build up a feeling of tension or suspense.**

> **Examiner's tip**
>
> In your answer you could include:
> - how the threatening situation developed: did the threat occur suddenly or did it come about gradually?;
> - how the characters felt at different stages of the occasion;
> - dramatic re-creation of moments of fear;
> - significant details of the place, people and events in the situation;
> - how the situation was resolved – if at all.

OR

b You decide to form a group at your school to support a charitable organisation. This could be for Young Amnesty or some other cause you feel strongly about. Your aim is to involve people in raising money and joining in activities.

> **Write an article for your school newsletter, explaining what you plan to do and why.**

You could write about:

- reasons why you want to support this cause;
- activities you are hoping to organise;
- ways of raising money to support the organisation;
- how you want people to support your activities.

Paper 2
Shakespeare

Instructions to student

- This test is 1 hour 15 minutes long.

- Paper 2 is based on the three Shakespeare extracts on pages 5–11 in the English booklet.

- You should do the task for **one** of the following plays:

  Romeo and Juliet

  Macbeth

  Twelfth Night

- Write your answer on separate paper.

- Your work will be assessed for your knowledge and understanding of the play and the way you express your ideas. Your spelling and handwriting will also be assessed.

- You will gain extra credit if you:
  – use details and quotations from the scene to support your ideas;
  – comment on the language of the characters;
  – refer to other parts of the play when they fit in with your answer;
  – write about it as drama (part of a play written and performed for an audience).

- Check your work carefully.

Start		Finish	

Choose **ONE** task.

EITHER

Romeo and Juliet
Act 1 Scene 5, Lines 39–125

1 In this part of the play Romeo and Juliet meet for the first time and fall in love. It is love at first sight for both of them. Romeo has 'gatecrashed' the Capulet party. For this task you are asked to choose any one of the characters present at this party. You observe what happens and later write about it in your diary.

> **Imagine that you are one of the characters in this scene. Write in your diary what you have noticed happen and what your feelings are.**

Before you begin to write you should think about:

- the best choice of character (i.e. which character would have noticed the most and experienced the greatest range of emotions?);

- Romeo and Juliet falling in love at first sight;

- the language used by the important characters;

- some of the things that have happened before this scene.

OR

Macbeth
Act 1 Scene 7

2   This is the scene in which Macbeth struggles with his conscience, loses the struggle and so chooses his fate. Macbeth's fate will be a tragic one because his ambition allows Lady Macbeth to influence him against his own, better, judgement. At this point in the play Shakespeare presents Macbeth as a hero with a choice; a hero loved and trusted by Duncan.

38
Q2

> **Show how Macbeth struggles with his conscience and the important part played by Lady Macbeth in this scene.**

Before you begin to write you should consider:

- what has happened in the play before this scene;

- Macbeth's arguments against killing Duncan (lines 3–28);

- what Lady Macbeth says when Macbeth tells her he has changed his mind (lines 35–60);

- the way the murder will be carried out (lines 60–70).

Paper 2

OR

Twelfth Night
Act 1 Scene 5, Lines 136–253

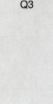

38

Q3

3 Viola (disguised as Cesario) enters. She has come to woo Olivia on behalf of Orsino.

> **What more does the audience learn about Olivia and Viola in this part of the play?**

Before you begin to write you should think about:

- the situation;

- what more we learn about the two characters;

- what is interesting and entertaining for the audience;

- the way language is used.

How to approach Paper 1

These questions don't ask you to do anything which has not been part of your studies at Key Stage 3.

You will have had many opportunities to develop as an effective reader: decoding signs; interpreting clues; grappling with language, form and ideas; and understanding the purposes of writers and the audiences for whom they are writing. This is just another opportunity to show what you can do.

Notice that the marks available for Questions 1–3 vary. Bear this in mind when doing this practice test, and also when you tackle the real thing. Try to divide your time accordingly. Ideally, an answer with 11 marks should take almost twice as long to construct as one with 6 marks (this does not mean that your answer has to *be* twice as long). In a test situation it doesn't always work out so simply; don't spend too much test time looking at your watch!

Examiner's tip

Your answers to these questions will all benefit from thorough and skim reading. Do not be afraid to write on the passages in the booklet:

- use subheadings;
- underline key words and sentences;
- circle relevant phrases, sentences or images;
- divide the text into sections;
- make brief notes.

SECTION C

Notice that there are 33 marks for this question. That's a little more than the total available for Sections A–B. Try to organise your time accordingly.

The examiner will be focused on the *quality* of your written response rather than the quantity. Treat this test as an opportunity to show what your teachers have helped you to learn about being a better writer. The test only offers you limited scope to do this – but this is true for everyone else who takes it.

At its best, your answer will confirm decisions your teacher has made about the developing quality of your work during Key Stage 3.

The following pages take you through how to approach each question in turn. Read this section before you attempt your own answers. When you have completed the test, turn to the Assessment Criteria for each question to discover how to mark your test. You will also find examples of how these criteria have been specifically applied to some sample answers. Read these sample answers and then mark your own test using the same criteria.

How to approach Section A   Question 1

REMINDER OF THE TASK
The first 61 lines describe what Andres sees and does.

Give your impressions of what is happening and how Andres is involved.

In your answer you should comment on:

- what is happening to the prisoners;

- what Andres does;

- what Andres thinks and feels.

You should support your ideas with words and phrases from the passage.

Examiner's tip

Notice details that help you to imagine what it is like for Andres to be in that situation. Refer to these details in your answer. Your answer should show the development in Andres' reactions to the changing situation. Keep your mind on the lead question and link your answer to this.

KEY POINTS
Your answer could refer to some of the following key points:

What is happening to the prisoners	What Andres does	What Andres thinks and feels
• the prisoners are beaten if they hesitate to leave the trucks;	• stays clear of the crowd;	• feels desperate to get through the crowd;
• Andres' friend jumps from the truck;	• watches the truck arrive;	• fears the American has a gun;
• the last prisoners are driven from the truck;	• sees his friend;	• feels a thrill of hope about the presence of a pressman;
• the guards beat one who is too slow.	• breaks forward, seeking a gap;	• forgets his own danger out of concern for his friend, Braulio.
	• follows the American;	
	• tells him the world's got to know;	
	• gets the crowd to part;	
	• accepts his camera.	

How to approach Section A   Question 2

REMINDER OF THE TASK

Read the rest of the passage from line 62 to the end. The soldiers become more violent and this is described in more detail. You may also notice, however, that Andres now has the means to reduce or even stop any more violence in the future.

Show how Andres is affected by the increasing danger and explain why there is a chance of doing something about stopping this violence in the future.

In your answer you should comment on:

- how the writer uses these details;
- the American photographer, his role and importance;
- the behaviour of the soldiers;
- Andres' reactions.

You should support your ideas with words and phrases from the passage.

Examiner's tip

Show that you understand:
- what the extract is about;
- what techniques the writer uses to build up a sense of danger;
- what techniques the writer uses to suggest a sense of hope.

Use examples from the text in your answer and try to explain their effect on the reader.

Do not just list the events. Try to show *how* the feeling of danger increases and *how* a sense of hope develops. Link your answer to the lead question.

KEY POINTS

Your answer could refer to some of the following key points:

The American photographer	The behaviour of the soldiers	Andres' reactions
• he cannot be saved by the crowd;	• their beating of the American photographer;	• initially a helpless onlooker;
• he is a victim of violence (answers may refer to how this is conveyed);	• their search for the camera;	• overcome by the strength of the Junta;
• the soldiers are searching for his camera;	• their flinging of the American photographer out of the Stadium.	• realisation that the film is important proof of the military's brutality;
• he is an American citizen (answers may develop the significance of this).		• witness of brutality to an American citizen;
		• new-found sense of purpose.

How to approach Section B   Question 3

REMINDER OF THE TASK

Read the Amnesty International pamphlet on pages 3–4 of the English booklet.

The leaflet is designed to persuade young people to join Amnesty International. Point out how it does so.

In your answer you should comment on:

- how the writer has selected information about Amnesty;

- the way words, layout and images are used in the leaflet to persuade you;

- whether you think the leaflet succeeds.

Examiner's tip

Try to show that you have identified the persuasive arguments in the leaflet. Comment on how pictures, presentation and the choice of language add to the impact of the leaflet.

KEY POINTS

Your answer could refer to some of the following key points:

Content and layout

- details of real life victims;

- pictures of young people;

- illustration of 'youth action' in the form of a badge;

- short factual paragraphs using dramatic language listing different kinds of torture;

- use of bold type to ask shocking questions which appear to be rhetorical but are about things which have actually happened;

- uses current examples;

- reader is shown how he/she can make a difference.

How and why Amnesty International is effective

- 96 countries no longer have capital punishment;

- publishes facts on torture and unfair imprisonment;

- highlights injustice to young people;

- the school girl, Nafije, was released from prison six months after Amnesty became involved;

- is independent of governments and is clear about its own principles on torture and the death penalty;

- organises letter-writing campaigns;

- the information on how the reader can help is written in the present tense.

How your joining Amnesty International can help

- you write directly to important politicians;

- you add your voice to others around the world;

- you can hire a video and/or do an assembly to raise others' awareness;

- you give hope to prisoners;

- you make prisoners feel less isolated;

- your donations help funding.

Paper 1 Answers

REMINDER OF THE TASK

Write about a threatening situation. You could write about a real or an imaginary event. Try to build up a feeling of tension or suspense.

In your answer you could include:

- how the threatening situation developed: did the threat occur suddenly or did it develop gradually?;

- how the characters felt at different stages of the occasion;

- dramatic re-creation of moments of fear;

- significant details of the place, people and events in the situation;

- how the situation was resolved – if at all.

Examiner's tip

In your answer you are being asked to:
- show that you can present content so as to engage and sustain the interest of the reader;
- structure sequences of events and ideas in ways that make meaning clear to a reader;
- sustain a chosen style;
- write accurately.

A well-structured piece of writing will be more successful than a long rambling one.
Try to remember the following when structuring your writing:
- aim for a strong beginning and a clear, shaped ending;
- paragraph your writing to indicate the main elements and turning points;
- vary your sentence structure;
- use a wide range of vocabulary;
- include appropriate detail to bring the writing alive;
- check your writing for spelling and punctuation.

KEY POINTS

Your answer will be improved if you:

Plan your writing

- choose a subject or setting with which you have some familiarity;

- centre your writing around a simple plot which shows how the situation developed;

- begin with an interesting opening;

- vary the pace and feature a small number of characters and a single setting;

- explore the changing emotions and feelings of the main characters;

- use interesting and varied language, including some dialogue, to convey significant details of places, people and events;

- try to end with some sort of self-knowledge or high/low points.

Paper 1 Answers

REMINDER OF THE TASK

You decide to form a group at your school to support a charitable organisation. This could be for Young Amnesty or some other cause you feel strongly about. Your aim is to involve people in raising money and joining in activities

Write an article for your school newsletter, explaining what you plan to do and why.

You could write about:

- reasons why you want to support this cause;

- activities you are hoping to organise;

- ways of raising money to support Amnesty International;

- how you want people to support your activities.

Examiner's tip

Responding successfully to this question involves clarity of thought, and persuasion of the reader. Your article should appeal to logic and emotion, and develop a sense of involvement. You need to assure people that this is a good course of action. There is no need to use headlines or sub-headings.

KEY POINTS

In your answer, you should try to:

- show that you can present content so as to engage and sustain the interest of the reader;

- structure sequences of events and ideas in ways that make the meaning clear to a reader;

- inform and persuade a specific audience;

- sustain a chosen style;

- write accurately.

Examiner's tip

Whichever part you choose to answer for Question 4 on this test, you may find it helpful to tackle the alternative on another occasion, to give yourself a chance to improve your ability to answer a different type of writing question. Remember, you complete this section at the end of Paper 1. You may become pressurised for time. However, you will be rewarded for what you have written even if your handwriting at the end is not as neat as it could be.

How to mark Paper 1

How to mark Section A   Question 1

The criteria that follow should be used to assess your answer for Question 1. Begin with the criteria for Level 4. If your answer meets at least two of these criteria, move on to consider the criteria for Level 5. Keep moving through the levels in this way for as long as you can identify these qualities in your response. Stop (or go back) when you feel you have reached the level that best describes your answer. Award your answer the relevant number of marks for that level, for example, 3 marks for a Level 5 answer. A sample answer on page 16 has been marked for you.

ASSESSMENT CRITERIA	Marks
LEVEL 4 • There may be a little explanation – showing some understanding of the main ideas. • The answer is mostly relevant, selecting facts and narrative which are relevant to the question. • There will be a few points with brief explanations, e.g. 'looks for his friend'. *Two or more criteria met? Check Level 5.* *Fewer than two? Award yourself 1 mark.*	2
LEVEL 5 • A fuller answer with linked explanations, showing more detailed understanding. • A competent, quite wide-ranging answer. • You cover the more obvious points, for example, you may explain the situation of the prisoners and provide some details of what Andres does. *Two or more criteria met? Check Level 6.* *Fewer than two? Go back to Level 4.*	3
LEVEL 6 • A better developed answer with some explanation. Points are sometimes developed in detail. • There is evidence of insight and involvement in seeing the situation from Andres' point of view. Relevant generalisations are made, e.g. 'Andres was feeling desperate'. • There is some understanding of what was behind Andres' concern. There may be some explanation for the changes in his behaviour, thoughts or feelings. • An answer at this level will be sustained by reference to the text and will relate the detail of what is happening to his thoughts and feelings. *Three or more criteria met? Check Level 7.* *Fewer than three? Go back to Level 5.*	4
LEVEL 7 • A good, reasonably full answer showing understanding of the text as a whole and closely linked to it. • Shows a clear grasp of more complex ideas such as the importance of the photographic evidence of brutality and the details of the text which convey this idea. • An overview is taken and different parts of the answer are linked. • Comments on the behaviour of other people are made relevant to Andres' reactions. *Three or more criteria met? Check Level 7+.* *Fewer than two? Go back to Level 6.*	5
LEVEL 7+ • A full appreciation of Andres' reactions. • Full and appropriate references to illustrate this. These references to the text are integrated into a detailed summary of the relationship between Andres' actions and his state of mind. *Both of these criteria met? Congratulations!* *If not, go back to Level 7.*	6

Ben's answer to Question 1

Consider this answer to Question 1, written by Ben, a Year 9 student. What level would you give it? Refer back to the assessment criteria on page 15.

The situation in which Andres finds himself is clearly so confused and chaotic that his feelings seem to change in each paragraph. This confusion is shown in the urgency of the language. The prisoners are being treated brutally. The brutality and its effects are described, for example: 'hastened on their way with rifle butts', '"Move, scum!"', 'A stream of blood had congealed down one side of his face', 'One was not fast enough to please his guards. He was hurt, hobbling, gripping his side in pain', 'A rifle butt swung against the stumbling prisoner'.

'Andres stayed clear of the crowd… Andres broke forward.' Andres tries to reach his friend and follows the tall American. He feels hopeful, for this is a journalist. He attracts the soldiers, giving the American a chance to photograph their brutality. He hides the American's camera for him.

When he sees Braulio, looking battered but unbowed, it makes him forget the danger he himself is in and push forward to help his friend. Similarly, his response to the arrival of Don Chailey begins with a fear that the American is armed and will attract danger, then changes to a near jubilation that an outsider is coming to aid the resistance and record the brutalities that are going on.

Since the passage is written largely from Andres' perspective it allows us to see the way in which his feelings are in chaos mirroring the chaos around him, and suggests the way in which danger and exhaustion heighten his emotions.

Assessment of Ben's answer

Compare Ben's answer to the key points on page 10 and the assessment criteria on page 15.

- He presents his ideas very confidently.
- He sets about answering the tasks quickly.
- He makes many relevant references to the extract.
- He is able to keep control of long sentences containing a number of ideas – look at the last sentence, for example.
- Despite the pressures of time, in his actual test answer Ben's handwriting was clear and his spelling and punctuation were mainly correct.
- His ideas are clearly connected using words such as 'this', 'then', 'when', 'similarly', 'since'.
- He doesn't simply retell the events of the passages.
- He explains how language is used.

Ben's piece merits Level 7+. He refers closely to the text, is sensitive to its inferences, has a clear grasp of complex ideas and links different parts of his answer to each other. Furthermore, he is aware of the way in which language is used to create effect.

How to mark Section A   Question 2

Use the criteria that follow to mark your answer to Question 2.

A sample answer on page 18 has been marked for you.

ASSESSMENT CRITERIA	Marks
LEVEL 4 • Little explanation, showing some understanding. • There will be *some* summary of the sources of danger and the chances of stopping it in the future, for example, a statement about the beating or the search for the camera. • There may be some reference to Andres' trembling. • There may be some grasp of the importance of the film. *Two or more criteria met? Check Level 5.* *Fewer than two? Award yourself 3 marks.*	**4**
LEVEL 5 • There will be some explanations, a number of points without much detail and a fuller understanding of the text. • The danger may be mentioned without much detail, so might the chances of stopping the violence – without a full explanation. • The answer will be built into a sequence of linked events. *Two or more criteria met? Check Level 6.* *Fewer than two? Go back to Level 4.*	**6**
LEVEL 6 • This answer will be better developed, with some exploration of the text; points will sometimes be developed in detail. • There will be an appreciation of how the writer introduces the chances of stopping the violence. • There may be explanation of how the violence is conveyed or understanding of how Andres would feel. • The answer will be supported by some reference to the text. *Three or more criteria met? Check Level 7.* *Fewer than three? Go back to Level 5.*	**8**
LEVEL 7 • A good answer showing clearly expressed understanding of the whole text and closely linked to it, in a detailed way, through reference or relevant quotations. • There is some understanding of *how* the writer conveys the danger and the feelings of hope. • The answer may identify the moment when everything changes, comment on the depiction of Andres' feelings and show how the events lead to an optimistic climax. *Two or more criteria met? Check Level 7+.* *Fewer than two? Go back to Level 6.*	**10**
LEVEL 7+ • A full answer clearly focused on how the writer achieves these effects. • There is discussion of *how* some aspects of language and structure build up tension. • References are used skilfully, to justify comments. *All three criteria met? Congratulations!* *If not, go back to Level 7.*	**11**

Paper 1 Answers

Now consider this answer to Question 2, also written by Ben. What level would you give it? Refer to the assessment criteria on page 17.

The danger is shown in a vivid description of the soldiers attacking the American. His head is unprotected, in contrast to the soldiers, who wear helmets. The boots are iron clad against the vulnerable body, head and hands. Individuals in the crowd are endangered as the soldiers use violence in their efforts to find the camera. The author makes time stand still for Andres. He uses a vivid simile, 'trembled as if touched by an electrified fence', to show Andres' state of shock. He juxtaposes the vulnerability of an individual with the strong brutality of an armed dictatorship.

The American photographer is being attacked by the soldiers because they know how damaging the pictures are. They are searching for the camera and do not know that Andres has it. This is Andres' chance to do something that will affect the future behaviour of the soldiers. He knew that what was in the camera was just as valuable as bullets. The pictures were proof of the soldiers' brutality towards an American citizen. Suddenly Andres has a chance of stopping any more of this violence in the future. He is not just another face in the crowd: 'All at once he had a purpose, a direction, a next step.'

Assessment of Ben's answer

Ben's answer to Question 2, although briefer, concentrates on the key words of the question – 'danger' and 'stopping this violence'. Check his answer against the key points on page 11 and the assessment criteria on page 17.

Ben refers economically to a number of important points. He does not get drawn into long repetition of the text, choosing instead to give an overview of the important points.

- He recognises the significance of the American photographer and his camera.
- He shows how Andres' reactions change.
- He recognises the relationship between the power of the soldiers and the confusion amongst the people.

Ben's answer to Question 2 is as good as his answer to Question 1. He shows an understanding of the significance of the passage and the techniques used by the writer, such as description, juxtaposition and simile. There is appreciation of the writing as a whole and relevant reference to the text. Although this answer is not as long as his answer to Question 1, it is of a very high quality – a Level 7+ is appropriate.

How to mark Section B	Question 3

Use the following assessment criteria to mark your answer to Question 3.

A sample answer on page 20 has been marked for you.

ASSESSMENT CRITERIA	Marks
LEVEL 4 • Little explanation. Some of the main factual points are mentioned and simple deductions are made, for example: 'people imprisoned, tortured, executed'. • You have referred to the text, but in an unfocused way, for example, by writing out sections of the text without linking them to your comments. • You refer broadly, but not necessarily directly, to the ways the pamphlet tries to persuade. *Two or more criteria met? Check Level 5.* *Fewer than two? Award yourself 3 marks.*	4
LEVEL 5 • Some understanding of the methods used by the text. • Points selected and commented on, perhaps with simple suggestions regarding their effectiveness. • The general effect of language, layout or pictures may be described. • There is an overview of Amnesty International's work which may not always be closely linked to the text. *Three or more criteria met? Check Level 6.* *Fewer than three? Go back to Level 4.*	6
LEVEL 6 • A better developed answer with some explanation of the text. • There is a clear grasp of the contents of the pamphlet, the need for Amnesty International and how the pamphlet persuades people. Appropriate references support this. • There may be recognition of less obvious features, for example the use of headlines, short paragraphs, photographs, extracts from the lives of victims. • There may be further examples of layout and illustration and why these are effective. *Three or more criteria met? Check Level 7.* *Fewer than three? Go back to Level 5.*	8
LEVEL 7 • A confident, reasonably full answer showing a grasp of the whole text and closely and appropriately linked to it. • Questions are answered directly, with clear links to the pamphlet. • Points are made and explained in some detail with examples and judgements of effectiveness. • There are references to the writer's use of language. • Different parts of the answer are linked. *Three or more criteria met? Check Level 7+.* *Fewer than three? Go back to Level 6.*	10
LEVEL 7+ • A full answer which analyses the text and shows appreciation of its persuasive techniques. • You show evaluation of the pamphlet's approach by selecting ideas and discussing how they are conveyed. • Skilfully selected references justify the responses. *All three criteria met? Outstanding performance!* *If not, go back to Level 7.*	11

Ben's answer to Question 3

Here is Ben's answer to Question 3. Refer back to the assessment criteria on page 19 and decide at which level you would place this answer.

This leaflet contains stories of real-life victims of torture, death penalties and being in prison. Photos of young victims, one only 12, are printed. Two of the three are dead now.

There are questions with short, high-impact answers. The questions are brutally direct. They are in the past tense. The impact is increased by this, the reader can do nothing about this injustice. It has already taken place.

Questions contain the word <u>you</u>. They ask <u>you</u> to put yourself in the place of the victims. The biggest printed question is 'Would you be put in prison if you complained about your school?' This possibility shakes the reader.

A variety of typeface is used. Some, in block capitals, lists the ways Amnesty responds, e.g. by 'Campaigning for the release of prisoners of conscience'. These are in the present tense – action that is happening now.

Amnesty's work is shown to be effective, 96 countries no longer have capital punishment. The girl imprisoned for complaining about school was released after Amnesty's involvement. This is 'Stop Press' next to a 'Youth Action' badge. Her friends are still in prison. Turning over, the reader can find out how, through youth action, he or she can help the prisoners and other victims. This section is more formal – it emphasises Amnesty's independence and effectiveness and tells of ways the reader can be involved in Amnesty's work by joining. We are to send NOW for more information. Now is in capitals – all the goals and means of achieving them are in block capitals. The headlines stating the problems are in lower case.

The leaflet does not patronise the reader. Overall it is very effective.

Assessment of Ben's answer

This is a very good answer which deals with all aspects of the question. Ben describes what is in the leaflet and points out how the images used have an emotional impact on the reader. For example, the effective use of photographs because two of the three people are now dead. He shows how the use of language supports and increases the effectiveness of the writing. It is an analytical answer which explains by appropriate references, for example, the underlining of the word 'you', how certain grammatical features support the effect and meaning of the writing. He shows how the use of the present tense in the block capital headlines tells the reader that the work of Amnesty is going on now.

The response to the typeface/font of the headline shows an awareness of how presentation contributes to meaning. Ben also understands how the structure and layout of the leaflet leads the reader into becoming involved. This answer merits Level 7+

Examiner's tip

Remember, Questions 1–3 assess reading, not writing. Even if your answer is not expressed perfectly, you will gain marks if you show evidence of your understanding.

Paper 1 Answers

Use the assessment criteria on page 22 if you answered part a; use the criteria on page 23 if you answered part b. Decide which level best describes your writing following the steps below. Then award yourself the relevant number of marks, according to how well you feel your writing meets the criteria, as described below. Begin with the questions for Level 4.

- If you are only able to answer 'yes' to fewer than half the questions for Level 4, you may be at an earlier stage of development and working at Level 3.

  Award yourself 6 marks total.

- If you are able to answer 'yes' to more than half the questions for Level 4, go on to consider the questions for Level 5. If you then answer 'yes' to fewer than half the questions for Level 5, you are probably working at Level 4.

  Award yourself 12 marks total.

- If you are able to answer 'yes' to more than half of the Level 5 questions, you are probably working at Level 5.

  Award yourself 18 marks total.

- If you are able to answer 'yes' to most of the questions for Level 5, go on to consider the questions for Level 6. If you then answer 'yes' to fewer than half of the Level 6 questions, you are probably working at Level 5.

  Award yourself 18 marks total.

- If you are able to answer 'yes' to at least half of the Level 6 questions, then you are probably working at Level 6.

  Award yourself 24 marks total.

- If you are able to answer 'yes' to most of the questions for Level 6, go on to consider the Level 7 questions. If you then answer 'yes' to only one or two questions for Level 7, you are probably working at Level 6.

  Award yourself 24 marks total.

- If you are able to answer 'yes' to at least half of the questions for Level 7, then you are probably working at Level 7.

  Award yourself 30 marks total.

- If you are able to answer 'yes' to most of the questions for Level 7, go on to consider the questions for Level 7+. If you then answer 'yes' to fewer than half of these questions, you are probably working at Level 7.

  Award yourself 30 marks total.

- If you are able to answer 'yes' to most or all of the questions for Level 7+, you are probably working at a High Level 7 or above.

  Award yourself 33 marks total.

A sample answer to Question 4a has been marked for you on pages 24–5.

A sample answer to Question 4b has been marked for you on pages 26–7.

ASSESSMENT CRITERIA FOR QUESTION 4a	Yes	No
LEVEL 4		
Is the overall structure of the writing sound, shown by the clear movement from beginning to end in narrative writing?	☐	☐
Are the ideas generally presented in a way which makes them easy to follow?	☐	☐
Does the writing begin to have descriptive words used effectively?	☐	☐
Is the spelling generally accurate?	☐	☐
Are there signs of a shift from simple sentence structure to the the use of complex sentences, properly punctuated?	☐	☐
Is the handwriting mostly clear and legible?	☐	☐
Is there some use of paragraphs?	☐	☐
LEVEL 5		
Does the writing describe such things as feelings, characters and settings?	☐	☐
Are words used precisely?	☐	☐
Is paragraphing used to make the movement of the narrative clear?	☐	☐
Is punctuation used accurately, including the use of apostrophes, quotation marks and commas?	☐	☐
Is a wide range of vocabulary evident and generally spelt accurately?	☐	☐
Is the handwriting generally clear, legible and fluent?	☐	☐
LEVEL 6		
Does the writing show an ability to engage and sustain the reader's interest?	☐	☐
Is there a range of vocabulary and varied sentences (simple and complex) contributing to the quality of the writing?	☐	☐
Are other narrative aspects used, such as dialogue and scene-setting?	☐	☐
Is spelling accurate, though there may be some errors in difficult words?	☐	☐
Are punctuation and paragraphing used to good effect?	☐	☐
Is the handwriting consistently legible and fluent?	☐	☐
LEVEL 7		
Does the writing display a more assured use of narrative style?	☐	☐
Are the characters and settings developed, rather than just mentioned?	☐	☐
Is there evidence of an insight into motive and behaviour?	☐	☐
Does the overall structure show a range of approaches?	☐	☐
Does sentence structure vary according to purpose?	☐	☐
Are paragraphing and correct punctuation used to make the sequence of events clear?	☐	☐
Is vocabulary expressive and well chosen?	☐	☐
Is spelling correct, including that of complex irregular words?	☐	☐
Is the handwriting consistently legible and fluent?	☐	☐
LEVEL 7+		
Is the writing consciously crafted (i.e. control of feelings, characters, events and settings)?	☐	☐
Do vocabulary and grammar make fine distinctions and emphasise viewpoint?	☐	☐
Is the punctuation, spelling and paragraphing almost faultless?	☐	☐
Is the handwriting consistently clear and fluent?	☐	☐
Are originality and creativity shown?	☐	☐

ASSESSMENT CRITERIA FOR QUESTION 4b	Yes	No
LEVEL 4 Are the ideas generally clear with some appropriate organisation?	☐	☐
Is there some attempt to persuade the reader?	☐	☐
Are the ideas presented in a lively and thoughtful manner, with an appropriate choice of vocabulary?	☐	☐
Is the spelling of commonly used words generally accurate?	☐	☐
Are there signs of a shift from simple sentence structure to the use of complex sentences, properly punctuated?	☐	☐
Is the handwriting mostly clear and legible?	☐	☐
LEVEL 5 Is there variety in the writing, both in sentence structure and in the shaping of the overall structure of the piece?	☐	☐
Are words used precisely with paragraphing used to make the movement of the persuasive argument clear?	☐	☐
Is punctuation used accurately, including the use of apostrophes, quotation marks and commas?	☐	☐
Is reasonably wide vocabulary used?	☐	☐
Is handwriting generally clear and legible in a fluent style?	☐	☐
Is spelling, including that of complex patterns, mostly accurate?	☐	☐
LEVEL 6 Is the informative/argumentative writing sophisticated, showing the ability to engage and sustain the reader's interest?	☐	☐
Are sentences varied in length and structure for particular effect; is paragraphing generally appropriate?	☐	☐
Are other aspects of non-fiction writing used, such as analysis, clear layout and reflection?	☐	☐
Is spelling accurate on the whole, including that of irregular words?	☐	☐
Is punctuation used to good effect in sentences, with intelligent use of paragraphs?	☐	☐
LEVEL 7 Does the writing display a more assured use of expository or argumentative style?	☐	☐
Is the sense of audience clear, with various devices used to set out a case, for example, the anticipation of objections to an argument?	☐	☐
Does the overall structure show a range of approaches with sentence structure and paragraphing varying according to purpose?	☐	☐
Is punctuation accurate and vocabulary expressive and well chosen?	☐	☐
Is spelling correct, including that of complex irregular words?	☐	☐
Is the writing legible and attractively presented?	☐	☐
LEVEL 7+ Are the ideas clearly presented in a way which involves the reader's interest and keeps it throughout?	☐	☐
Is there a sense of balance, with just enough said and everything relevant?	☐	☐
Is the meaning clear, with emphasis made clearly and appropriately?	☐	☐
Is the spelling correct, including that of complex irregular words, and is the handwriting fluent and legible?	☐	☐
Is there excellent use of punctuation and paragraphing?	☐	☐

Carrie's answer to Question 4a

Read Carrie's answer to Question 4a. What level do you think it would be? Refer to the assessment criteria on page 22.

We'd been living in the valley for about 8 years before it happened. The old barn had been completely rebuilt by my parents, using local materials and craftsmen. As a family we had been happy to leave the bustle of Birmingham and make a new life in the rural west of Wales. Mum's job as a translator could be easily done from home and Dad was happy with our fields and sheep, and restoring old furniture.

Everything was fine. The locals were friendly and it had been fun to learn Welsh in school.

Yes, everything was fine until that spring morning. The tides were unusually high, the rainfall was unending.

It came on the news but we already knew. This would be the last night that anyone in our village would be able to stay in their own homes. The constant torrents of heavy rain had caused the river to rise ever higher, the danger ever closer.

It was at a point that was maybe eight hours before it broke through the barriers, but the way it was rising, it seemed like it wouldn't last four, let alone eight. Mum decided that we wouldn't risk staying.

All our most precious belongings had been stored upstairs. We prayed that those would be safe – we knew no one local would loot them, and hoped no strangers would be around. It seemed unlikely, given the weather!

Dad had the Land Rover running as we crammed ourselves, the two dogs, sleeping bags and spare clothing into the back. The sheep and early lambs had been taken to temporary barns further up the valley sides. Dad was torn between driving us to safety and staying with them.

Safety! We still had to travel along the road by the foaming torrents that formed the once placid Dovey river. Visibility was down to the minimum, the faster the wipers moved the more the rain seemed to block our view of what might lay ahead.

Our progress seemed painfully slow – he kept to the crest of where he thought the road may be, along the valley towards the tiny church at the top of the hill.

Dad knew he must keep the motor running. Fortunately this ex-Army Land Rover had a vertical exhaust, but it was still touch and go. None of the children spoke – leaving him to drive and Mum to 'navigate'.

'We should have bought a boat,' he muttered.

Soon the worst was over. The church, like a beacon, called us ever closer to its welcome light. It had been specially opened up for all who lived on the river banks, a refuge in case the barriers should burst and flood our homes.

By morning the church was crammed full. The river had flooded most of the village and we were marooned on this hilltop. I thought of our barn and how eight years of work would now be ruined, the belongings we hadn't been able to move floating around.

Ours was a strong community. People shared any food they had brought, calor gas heaters added to the radiators of the church.
We had faced danger and survived!

Assessment of Carrie's answer

Carrie's answer to Question 4a achieves a Level 7+ for a number of reasons:

- she shows a confident, assured style;

- the drama is well developed, building up from the calm, stable setting 'until that spring morning';

- character is not only well depicted at the start, but is developed throughout the piece;

- there is a strong sense of the nature of community and of the subtle differences between life in Birmingham and life in the Welsh countryside;

- the writing is well paragraphed – on the whole paragraphs are short, but dialogue is correctly presented and the momentum of the narrative is well served by the paragraphing;

- punctuation is largely accurate – there is use of complex, compound and simple sentence structure, all well punctuated;

- spelling is accurate;

- vocabulary is well chosen, ranging from the formal ('visibility was down to the minimum') to the colloquial ('the church was crammed full') in a natural, seemingly effortless way;

- there is variation in narrative voice: 'Yes, everything was fine...', 'We prayed that those would be safe...', 'Dad knew he must keep the motor running', 'By morning the church was crammed full', and 'I thought of our barn...'.

Aimee's answer to Question 4b

This answer to Question 4b was written by Aimee, a Year 9 student. It is reproduced here in her actual handwriting. What level do you think it would attain? Refer to the assessment criteria on page 23.

We have decided to form a Young Amnesty International group to try and help people from all over the world who are victims of cruel governments.

Our main reason is to raise money to support Amnesty and to form a letter writing group. If lots of individuals from all over the world who are writing to governments who torture people and put them in prison for their views then the governments might take notice, the prisoners will not feel forgotten.

We hope to organise a number of activities :- Cluedo (the life size version), a talent contest and various sponsored events to raise money for our group.

Quite a number of our year group are planning to raise money. One girl is being sponsored to try and conquer her fear of snakes by sitting for two hours with a snake around her neck! We are also holding a car wash day. We hope that you will sponsor some of the events arranged and come to have your car washed.

The problem of political prisoners exists all around the world. Amnesty is in desperate need of funds and supporters and deserves your help. I know that there are a lot of deserving causes but I think that this is a chance for us to help suffering people around the world Not only will you and ourselves be

raising money, we will be actively involved in letter writing. You are welcome to join us - assisting in our events, and if you would like to, writing letters.
The 'Cluedo' event is on the 12th of May, the snake sit in takes place on the same day.
A sponsor form is attatched.

Assessment of Aimee's answer

This is an interesting article. We learn about Amnesty International, fundraising and how the reader can be involved. The reader's interest is sustained by her approach. Particularly good aspects are:

- Some planning has gone on – the clear structure is designed to achieve the purposes outlined in the question.

- A short introductory paragraph states the article's purpose. The second paragraph summarises the work of Amnesty. Paragraphs three and four explain the fundraising activities. Paragraph five underlines and personalises the need for such an organisation. Paragraph six also aims to involve the reader. Necessary factual information is given in the remaining paragraphs.

- Aimee has used a range of persuasive phrases which have an emotional impact, for example 'cruel governments', 'who torture people', 'suffering people'.

- She meets people's objections to the singling out of Amnesty as an object for their charity, building up a sense of personal involvement and a sense of people acting together, for example, 'a chance for us to help', 'actively involved', 'welcome to join us'.

- She puts her views forward with clarity and coherence. Her sentences show variety. They often contain more than one idea when this is appropriate and they are easy to understand. There is a range of punctuation, helpfully and accurately used.

- Whenever it is appropriate each paragraph refers back to and develops what has gone before. There are a number of appealing sentences. She seems to be very able to use a range of vocabulary which is appropriate for her purposes. The ending is rather abrupt; this could be due to pressure of time.

- Handwriting and spelling produced under examination conditions cannot be expected to be anyone's best. Aimee's spelling (including irregular words except for 'attached') is generally accurate. Her work is neat and legible.

Such achievements would be likely to receive a mark within the Level 7+ range.

How to approach Paper 2

As with Paper 1, it is important to think through your answer to Paper 2, the Shakespeare paper. You only have to answer one question. Choose a question for the play you have studied: *Romeo and Juliet* or *Macbeth* or *Twelfth Night*.

During your work at school on the set play, you will have had many opportunities to demonstrate your writing and reading skills. Many of these involved the drafting and redrafting of your answers. You will also have read the whole play and had a chance to develop a sense of the plot; establish for yourself the main characters and their characteristics; and work out how the chosen lines relate to the whole play. Think about the main themes and other aspects, like the dramatic tension and the language used. You may even have acted parts out at school or seen a production.

For this test, you will have to pace your writing so that you answer as well as you can within the time limit. You are asked to complete one task in relation to one extract. The Shakespeare paper is designed to assess your ability to understand and respond to:

- Shakespeare's presentation of ideas;

- the motivation and behaviour of characters;

- the development of the plot;

- the language of the scene you choose;

- the overall impact of the scene you choose;

- the presentation of the scenes on stage.

It is also designed to assess your ability to:

- write in a style appropriate to the task;

- organise writing clearly, using paragraphs where appropriate;

- use grammatical structures and vocabulary suitable for the clear expression of meaning;

- use a variety of sentence structures;

- use accurate punctuation and spelling;

- write clearly and legibly.

Examiner's tip

The best way to start your answer is to re-read the extract to remind yourself of its qualities and of its place in the play. You should then look again at the task and note the key words in it: what exactly is it asking you to look at and comment on? The next stage is to make notes, then to organise the main elements of your answer. You can make notes on the text, by underlining or circling important passages and lines. Such preparation will help you write a better answer.

The following pages take you through how to approach each question in turn. Read the approach for the task you have selected first. This section will give you pointers about what you should include in your answer. Then turn to the relevant assessment criteria for your question. You will find an example of how these criteria have been specifically applied to a model answer. Read the model answer and commentary, and then mark your test using the same criteria.

Paper 2 Answers

REMINDER OF THE TASK

In this part of the play Romeo and Juliet meet for the first time and fall in love. It is love at first sight for both of them. Romeo has 'gatecrashed' the Capulet party. For this task you are asked to choose any one of the characters present at this party. You observe what happens and later write about it in your diary.

Imagine that you are one of the characters in this scene. Write in your diary what you have noticed happen and what your feelings are.

Before you begin to write you should think about:

- the best choice of character (i.e. which character in the scene would have noticed the most and experienced the greater range of emotions?);

- Romeo and Juliet falling in love at first sight;

- the language used by the important characters;

- some of the things that have happened before this scene.

Examiner's tip

You need to tell the story of what happens in this scene from the point of view of the character you have chosen. You have to imagine yourself in that character's place and write in a personal style. However, as well as re-telling the story you have to point out the kind of language and imagery written by Shakespeare for your chosen character to speak. Do not be afraid to use your imagination. You should be able to include some of the language in this scene as part of your diary. Remember, there are intense and contradictory emotions swirling through the scene that will be experienced by the character you choose to imagine.

KEY POINTS

Your answer could include some of the following key points:

- the formal structure of an important speech between Romeo and Juliet;

- an understanding of some of the imagery created by the language;

- that the Capulets and Montagues are enemies;

- that the Montagues have no right to be at a Capulet party;

- that the love between Romeo and Juliet will turn out to be ill-fated.

How to approach Task 2   Macbeth

REMINDER OF THE TASK

This is the scene in which Macbeth struggles with his conscience, loses the struggle and so chooses his fate. Macbeth's fate will be a tragic one because his ambition allows Lady Macbeth to influence him against his own, better, judgement. At this point in the play Shakespeare presents Macbeth as a hero with a choice; a hero loved and trusted by Duncan.

Show how Macbeth struggles with his conscience and the important part played by Lady Macbeth in this scene.

Before you begin to write you should consider:

* what has happened in the play before this scene;

* Macbeth's arguments against killing Duncan (lines 3–28);

* what Lady Macbeth says when Macbeth tells her he has changed his mind (lines 35–60);

* the way the murder will be carried out (lines 60–70).

Examiner's tip

The stage is busy with Macbeth's butler and servants preparing a hospitable and celebratory feast for Duncan, King of Scotland. This is Macbeth's castle. Macbeth enters by himself. He takes no notice of the work going on in the Great Hall because he is pre-occupied with thoughts of the consequences of murdering the King. He is struggling with his conscience. He decides not to kill Duncan. Lady Macbeth appears and he tells his wife that he has changed his mind. She is furious. She accuses him of being a coward and of not being a proper man. She outlines a plan that shows how easy it would be to kill Duncan and blame other people for the murder. Macbeth changes his mind again. His ambition and his wife's ambition will now lead them both along a bloody and a tragic path.

KEY POINTS

Your answer could include some of the following points:

* the idea that Macbeth chose his fate and his tragedy;

* an explanation of why Lady Macbeth was so angry with her husband;

* the part played by the Witches before this scene;

* the association of pity and fear with kindness and decent behaviour.

Paper 2 Answers

REMINDER OF THE TASK

Viola (disguised as Cesario) enters. She has come to woo Olivia on behalf of Orsino.

What more does the audience learn about Olivia and Viola in this part of the play?

Before you begin to write you should think about:

- the situation;
- what more we learn about the two characters;
- what is interesting and entertaining for the audience;
- the way language is used.

Examiner's tip

We already know quite a lot about Olivia at this stage in the play. She is the object of, but does not return, Duke Orsino's romantic fantasies. Like him she has a false view of self. She is exaggeratedly mourning her father and brother's deaths and rejecting pleasure and love. This is not her true nature and this is hinted at earlier in this scene when being teased by her fool, and in her dismissal of Malvolio as being 'sick of self-love'. The shipwrecked Viola (who does not yet know if her twin brother lives) is already deceiving Orsino in her disguise as a man. In this role she has found herself falling in love with him. In Shakespeare's time, Viola would have been played by a boy – adding to the audience's amusement, confusion and disquiet. She is the play's 'heroine', freeing Olivia and Orsino from their warped views of themselves. In this scene we see Viola (as Cesario) wooing Olivia on Orsino's behalf. The complications of disguise and deception are increased as Olivia falls in love with 'her'.

KEY POINTS

Your answer could refer to some of the following points:

- what we already know about each character;
- what Olivia and Viola have in common;
- how the themes of the play (e.g. disguise, illusion) are developed;
- how the behaviour of each woman changes;
- the variety of language used;
- the effect of disguise and illusion on the audience.

How to mark Paper 2

This paper will try to assess both your reading ability and your writing ability. Your reading will be assessed in terms of your understanding and response to the text. To mark your understanding and response, find the specific assessment criteria for the question you answered. Then use the general assessment criteria for written expression on pages 44–5 to mark this aspect of your answer. Enter your marks for Understanding and Response and Written Expression on the Marking Grid on page 46.

> **How to mark Task 1**   Romeo and Juliet

First, mark your understanding and response by considering the questions below:

SHAKESPEARE ASSESSMENT CRITERIA: UNDERSTANDING AND RESPONSE	Yes	No
Are Romeo, Juliet and Tybalt mentioned?	☐	☐
Has any reference been made to what has happened earlier in the play?	☐	☐
Does the diary entry make clear the important events of the scene?	☐	☐
Is it a good choice of character?	☐	☐
Has the answer been written from the character's point of view?	☐	☐
Have any references been made to some of the patterns of the language?	☐	☐
Have references been made to other important characters?	☐	☐
Is it clear that the Capulets and Montagues are enemies?	☐	☐
Have some of the actual words spoken by the characters been used?	☐	☐
Is there some indication that the love of Romeo and Juliet is ill-fated?	☐	☐
Does the answer show some understanding of Shakespeare's use of language?	☐	☐

Award yourself 2 marks for every assessment question for which you were able to respond 'yes' (22 marks total). The following chart will give you an indication of the level at which you are working, in terms of your understanding and response:

Your score	Level
2–4 marks	Level 3
6–8 marks	Level 4
10–12 marks	Level 5
14–16 marks	Level 6
18–20 marks	Level 7
22 marks	Level 7+

Enter your marks for Understanding and Response on the Marking Grid on page 46. Then mark your Written Expression using the general criteria on pages 44–5. Enter your marks for Written Expression on the Marking Grid on page 46. You will find that the following sample answer has been marked using the same criteria (see page 35).

32

Consider this answer to Task 1. Refer to the assessment criteria for Understanding and Response for this scene on page 32 and to the general assessment criteria for Written Expression on pages 44–5. What level do you think it deserves? The answer is assessed on page 35.

Dear Diary,

I am in love, and this is the only place I can reveal my real feelings. All my mopings over Rosaline were an illusion. I believed it was love but Benvolio's advice that I was to look at other girls was good. Rosaline was an unattainable infatuation. But I cannot tell Benvolio of my new love for she is a Capulet.

Yes, my new love is Lord and Lady Capulet's daughter, Juliet.

There has been yet another fight between we Montagues and those people today. The ancient grudge goes on and on. I do not want hatred, I want love.

I'll have to keep this a secret, more questions from Mother and Father seem certain. They must never know, they could never approve, the old cannot understand.

No, I cannot tell Benvolio, and yet, if he hadn't intercepted the invitation to the Capulets' ball I would not have met fair Juliet. I could not believe then that my love for Rosaline would ever change.

And I cannot tell Mercutio either. He scoffs at love and scoffs at dreams. Strangely I had not wanted to go to the ball because of my dream and yet I am so in love now. It was a premonition of bad things and yet I am now into something so good.

We were foolish to gatecrash. If spotted by such as Tybalt we would surely have a fight on our hands.

As the dancing began I caught sight of the beautiful Juliet. It was love at first sight, 'For ne'er saw I such beauty till this night'. She stood out from everyone, 'As a rich jewel in an Ethiop's ear'. She was bright and dazzling. Joy of joys I was able to speak with this beauty. I compared her to a shrine, to a saint, for love like this seems almost sacred.

We touched hands, 'palm to palm' and then our first kiss was like a holy prayer. We kissed again. 'By the book' was how she described my kissing. Was I too passionate or too cold? It truly was passion. My language was simple and direct and from the heart. How could it not be so to such an honest beauty as she? She is a shrine, saint like. I am so in love. It is all happening so quickly as though life is speeding up and yet time stood still as we kissed.

Each of us spoke in what sounded like a sonnet as we talked of our love in terms of religious devotion,

'If I profane thee with my unworthiest hand...'

I began for no one could be worthy of her. She continued the sonnet form. I had rhymed 'hand' and 'stand', 'this' and 'kiss'.

She repeated this last rhyming and added 'much' and 'touch'. To her 'too' I offered 'do'. To her 'prayer' I rhymed 'despair'.

Oh, I hope despair will not be the story of our love. For she is a Capulet and I am, as a Montague, one of her family's enemies.

Assessment of Sophie's answer to Task 1

UNDERSTANDING AND RESPONSE

Sophie's answer is quite short and very good.

She has chosen Romeo as her character. At first sight this character might be difficult to write a diary entry for. He plays such an important and active part in the scene that he might not have had time to notice anything else. In fact this answer shows that Romeo was a good choice. As a character keeping a diary he has much to write about. Much more, in fact, than a character like Tybalt, although Tybalt is better placed as an observer of events. Romeo can write about falling in love, how it happened and the swirls of emotion that he experiences.

So much happens to Romeo in this short scene. He forgets about Rosaline and falls completely in love with Juliet. He realises that he has fallen in love with the daughter of his enemy and she has fallen in love with him. He knows he has to keep his new love secret even from his friends and certainly from his parents.

Sophie writes about this very well. She notices the kind of language and imagery used by Shakespeare to describe this love. She recognises, and very cleverly incorporates, the hidden sonnet of Romeo and Juliet's conversation into the diary. She uses some of the language of the play which she clearly understands. The diary entry also recognises that Tybalt is a danger.

Now consider the Shakespeare Assessment Criteria on page 32. Sophie's answer meets all of the criteria and would therefore score 22 marks (Level 7+) for Understanding and Response.

WRITTEN EXPRESSION

The quality of expression in this answer is as high as the quality of Understanding and Response, as is demonstrated by the following positive features:

- clear use of paragraphs;
- clear expression of ideas;
- a clever use of short quotations;
- some of the imagery created by the language has been understood;
- the formal patterning of the important speech between Romeo and Juliet is shown;
- the use of the personal pronoun 'I' is appropriate for a diary entry;
- there is a range of accurate and helpful punctuation;
- simple and complex sentences have been used;
- the style of writing gives the impression that these are Romeo's thoughts (i.e. a relevant and consciously crafted style has been used).

Using the assessment criteria on pages 44–5 to give a separate mark for Written Expression, Sophie's answer would be awarded a high Level 7 (16 marks).

How to mark Task 2   Macbeth

First, mark your understanding and response by considering the questions below:

SHAKESPEARE ASSESSMENT CRITERIA: UNDERSTANDING AND RESPONSE	Yes	No
Are Macbeth, Lady Macbeth and Duncan mentioned?	☐	☐
Are there relevant references to what has gone on before and after this scene?	☐	☐
Does the answer explain why Macbeth does not want to kill Duncan?	☐	☐
Does the answer explain why Macbeth changes his mind?	☐	☐
Does the answer explain what Lady Macbeth says to her husband?	☐	☐
Does the answer explain how the murder is to be carried out?	☐	☐
Have the words 'ambition' and 'tragedy' been used about the play and Macbeth?	☐	☐
Have quotations been used to support what has been said?	☐	☐
Is there some understanding of the way language has been used?	☐	☐
Has the idea of conscience been written about?	☐	☐
Has the question of what kind of qualities make a man been mentioned?	☐	☐

Award yourself 2 marks for every assessment question for which you were able to respond 'yes' (22 marks total). The following chart will give you an indication of the level at which you are working, in terms of your understanding and response:

Your score	Level
2–4 marks	Level 3
6–8 marks	Level 4
10–12 marks	Level 5
14–16 marks	Level 6
18–20 marks	Level 7
22 marks	Level 7+

Enter your marks for Understanding and Response on the Marking Grid on page 46. Then assess your Written Expression using the general criteria on pages 44–5. Enter your marks for Written Expression on the Marking Grid on page 46. The following sample answer has been marked using the same criteria (see page 39).

Kelly's answer to Task 2

Consider this answer to Task 2. Refer to the assessment criteria for Understanding and Response for this scene on page 36 and to the general assessment criteria for Written Expression on pages 44–5. What level do you think it deserves? The answer is assessed on page 39.

Scene 7 starts with Macbeth, alone, struggling with his conscience. He is considering the consequences for himself in this life, 'We shall have judgement here.', of the assassination, the political murder, of Duncan. If there were to be no consequences '… here, upon this bank and shoal of time…' then he would take his chances about what might happen to him in the next life. This image of the events of life and time as a flowing river recurs later in the play when once again Macbeth consider his conscience in Act 3 Scene 4 and says to Lady Macbeth:

> '… I am in blood
> Stepped in so far that should I wade no more,
> Returning were as tedious as go o'er.'

But here in Act 1 Scene 7, Macbeth has not yet started 'wading in blood'. At this point in the play he appears to be choosing not to do so as he considers the common sense and practical reasons against murdering Duncan. He would have to guard against future vengeance. He is Duncan's subject and therefore owes him loyalty. He is his relative and as Duncan is also a guest in Macbeth's house his safety and comfort is Macbeth's double responsibility. Duncan is a good and virtuous king loved by heaven. There would be widespread grief in heaven and among the people when they heard of his murder:

> '… or heaven's cherubin horsed
> Upon the sightless couriers of the air,
> Shall blow the horrid deed in every eye,
> That tears shall drown the wind.'

When Macbeth tells Lady Macbeth that he has decided 'to proceed no further in this business' she furiously asks him a whole list of insulting, rhetorical questions. She accuses him of being a drunk daydreamer and too much of a coward to really become king.

To call Macbeth a coward when he has fought bravely against Scotland's enemies raises the question of what makes a man. Macbeth protests that, 'I dare do all that may become a man' and indeed the only time in the play where he shows any fear is just after he has murdered Duncan. He should have left the daggers in the room but is too frightened to look again on what he has done. The audience is likely to think that Macbeth is right to feel fear at the sight of murder. Fear, doubt and pity seem to be a necessary part of conscience. At this point in the play Lady Macbeth does not listen to her conscience. Later her conscience will be an important cause of her madness.

The image of pity 'like a naked, new born babe' used by Macbeth as a reason for not murdering Duncan is used as a startlingly cruel reproach against him by Lady Macbeth:

> 'I have given suck and know
> How tender 'tis to love the babe that milks me:
> I would, while it was smiling in my face,
> Have plucked my nipple from his boneless gums
> And dashed the brains out, had I so sworn
> As you have done to this.'

She feels no pity and no fear and does not consider failure. She outlines her plan for how Duncan can be murdered. The guards will be drugged and Duncan left asleep and unguarded:

> 'What cannot you and I perform upon
> Th'unguarded Duncan?'

Afterwards these guards can be blamed for the murder. Ambition leads Macbeth to agree to the murder of Duncan and to accept Lady Macbeth's idea of the qualities that make a man:

> 'Bring forth men-children only,
> For thy undaunted mettle should compose
> Nothing but males.

'The deceit and double-dealing that will now be necessary until the murder remind the audience of what Duncan said about the Thane of Cawdor:

> There's no art
> To find the mind's construction in the face.'

The murder of Duncan is caused by Macbeth's ambition. He has no other reason for the murder:

> 'I have no spur
> To prick the sides of my intent, but only
> Vaulting ambition'.

This is what makes the play a tragedy and causes the eventual downfall of Macbeth and Lady Macbeth.

Assessment of Kelly's answer to Task 2

UNDERSTANDING AND RESPONSE

Kelly's answer shows a good understanding of the importance of this scene in the play. She understands the part played by ambition in Macbeth's downfall and something of the way in which Shakespeare has written the tragedy. She knows that Macbeth's tragic flaw is ambition and that this flaw is made worse by Lady Macbeth's own ambition both for herself and her husband.

She is aware of the context of the scene in the development of the play. She gives an indication that she knows what has happened before by quoting Duncan's comment about Cawdor. This associates Macbeth with a previous traitor and connects Duncan's comment neatly to the new Thane of Cawdor who is, of course, now Macbeth himself. Kelly shows that she also knows what happens to Lady Macbeth later in the play.

Her answer is clear about Macbeth's reasons for not killing Duncan and shows how and why he is persuaded to change his mind. She is clear about the way the murder is planned by Lady Macbeth.

Her answer starts to consider the qualities of manliness through Lady Macbeth's eyes and makes very good use of appropriate quotations. She understands how language is used to create dramatic effects and recognises that certain images are important and reappear elsewhere in the play. Finally, Kelly is aware of possible effects on an audience.

Looking at the assessment criteria on page 36, it is possible to answer 'yes' to all 11 questions. Therefore, Kelly would score 22 marks (i.e. Level 7+) for Understanding and Response.

NOTE

Other possible questions about Act 1 Scene 7 might ask you to write from the point of view of either Macbeth or from the point of view of Lady Macbeth.

WRITTEN EXPRESSION

This is a well-written answer. It contains the following positive features:

- accurate and helpful punctuation;

- quite short appropriate quotations, in quotation marks and usually on separate lines;

- well handled, compound sentence structures: 'She feels no pity and no fear and does not consider failure.';

- accurate spelling;

- a varied choice of words.

Looking at the assessment criteria on pages 44–5, Kelly's answer would be awarded Level 7+ (i.e. 16 marks) for Written Expression.

How to mark Task 3   Twelfth Night

First, mark your understanding and response by considering the questions below:

SHAKESPEARE ASSESSMENT CRITERIA: UNDERSTANDING AND RESPONSE	Yes	No
Does the answer put the question in the context of the play so far?	☐	☐
Are relevant characters besides Olivia and Viola mentioned?	☐	☐
Are themes of deception and reality identified?	☐	☐
Is the changing character of Olivia explained with examples?	☐	☐
Is Viola's character explored with examples?	☐	☐
Does the answer explain how an audience might view this scene?	☐	☐
Is the importance of acting referred to?	☐	☐
Is there consideration of the effect of Viola on Olivia?	☐	☐
Is there consideration of Viola's interest in Olivia?	☐	☐
Is there an understanding of the different ways language is used?	☐	☐
Are the ideas supported by relevant references and quotations?	☐	☐

Award yourself 2 marks for every assessment question to which you were able to respond 'yes' (22 marks total). The following chart will give you an indication of the level at which you are working, in terms of your understanding and response:

Your score	Level
2–4 marks	Level 3
6–8 marks	Level 4
10–12 marks	Level 5
14–16 marks	Level 6
18–20 marks	Level 7
22 marks	Level 7+

Enter your marks for Understanding and Response on the Marking Grid on page 46. Then assess your Written Expression using the general criteria on pages 44–5. Enter your marks for Written Expression on the Marking Grid on page 46. The following sample answer has been marked using the same criteria.

Thomas' answer to Task 3

Consider this answer to Task 3. Refer to the assessment criteria for Understanding and Response for this scene on page 40 and to the general assessment criteria for Written Expression on pages 44–5. What level do you think it deserves? The answer is assessed on page 43.

Already in this scene we have seen Olivia's enjoyment of her fool's wordplay and her sharpness with the self-loving Malvolio. This helps prepare us for what is to come as our curiosity is built up for the meeting of Viola and Olivia. They have in common letters of their name and both are playing roles – one a man, one a mourner – protecting themselves from male interest.

We have heard that Olivia is young, beautiful and rich, that Duke Orsino thinks he loves her, that she rejects him and, according to her uncle, Sir Toby, will not marry anyone more wealthy, powerful, older or cleverer than herself. The audience know much about Viola; a shipwreck victim who may have lost her brother, pluckily making a new life in disguise. She too is attractive but is poor. She is more practical than Olivia.

The audience sees the play's theme of deception and identity in the veiling of Olivia before Viola's entrance. She has come to woo Olivia on behalf of Orsino, her master. Later the face will be unveiled. How 'real' is what is revealed?

'We will draw a curtain and show you the picture', but can we trust what we see? Viola's 'I am not that I play' echoes this.

Olivia is going to come out of hiding and open herself to love and all that threatens. Viola will cure her of self-indulgent, self-deceiving love. Viola begins her speech (as Cesario) in over-flattering, over-complex language: 'Most radiant, exquisite and unmatchable beauty.' Unsure of who she is talking to (because of the veil) she never completes the speech so carefully prepared (perhaps by Orsino to whom she is loyal throughout the play) and lets her true nature show.

There is a dialogue of curiosity about each other:

> *'Whence come you sir?'*
> *'Are you a comedian?'*
> *'Are you the lady of the house?'*

The audience know the answers, the characters don't.

The two go on to play word games together, references to 'sail', 'swabber' and 'hull' repeating images of the sea – the means by which Viola has arrived in Illryia.

Olivia has vowed to mourn her dead brother and avoid men for seven years, but Viola's liveliness and energy win such a positive response that Olivia lifts her veil. Olivia also reveals a high opinion of her own good looks:

> *'Is't not well done?'*

Her thoughts and feelings are not so sad as she has pretended; Viola's language and appearance are winning Olivia over. Heightened poetical language, the traditional language of love, contrasts with Olivia's prose and Viola's moving and sincere lines beginning: 'Make me a willow cabin at your gate', show Olivia and the audience what love is really like. We recognise how honest she is and her good sense in expressing the sincerity of love.

Olivia and Viola are fascinated by one another, the audience are fascinated by the illusion and delusions presented in the play. Acting and people as actors, assuming roles and masking their true selves, are central to our enjoyment of the play. Olivia has moved on in this world. She has looked Viola up and down and is physically attracted as well as having enjoyed her language:

> 'Thy tongue, thy face, thy limbs, actions, and spirit
> Do give thee fivefold blazon.'

'Thou' and 'thy' were words used to show you felt close to people. Olivia realises the speed of her infatuation:

> 'Not too fast! Soft, soft!'

She associates love with sickness:

> 'Even so quickly may one catch the plague?'

Love has changed her perceptions as she thinks about the 'man' that she has just met. The audience will be developing and changing their perceptions of the characters.

> 'Me thinks I feel this youth's perfections
> With an invisible and subtle stealth
> To creep in at mine eyes.'

Viola's good looks, good humour and imaginative complements and sincerity have released the self-repressed Olivia's capacity for love.

Assessment of Thomas' answer to Task 3

UNDERSTANDING AND RESPONSE

This is an excellent answer. It shows a grasp of motivation and behaviour. It is a personal view based on thorough knowledge of the play. The final 'summing up' sentence shows this: 'Viola's good looks, good humour and imaginative compliments and sincerity have released the self-repressed Olivia's capacity for love.'

His understanding of the situation is shown in Thomas' first two paragraphs. He recounts what we already know about Olivia and Viola very economically and develops ideas about these characters which are relevant to the extract studied and the question answered. He helps the reader understand the situation. He does not spend too long giving evidence to back this excellent summary. He is right not to; he has more time to answer the question.

He skilfully links his account of the scene with very important themes of the play: deception, illusion and identity. His grasp of this is supported by appropriate quotations. In writing about the characters in this part of the play, he is able to identify the effect Viola is going to have on Olivia: 'Viola will cure her of self-indulgent, self-deceiving love'.

Thomas shows how double meaning and disguise will be enjoyed by the audience: 'The audience know the answers, the characters don't.' An examiner will be impressed by his grasp of the play as a performance, e.g. 'We recognise …', 'The audience will be developing …'.

Throughout his response, Thomas identifies the ways language is used, e.g. 'dialogue of curiosity', 'the two go on to play word games together', 'images of the sea', 'heightened poetical language', '"thou" and "thy"… show you felt close to people.'

He recognises double meaning, explaining, 'We will draw a curtain and show you the picture', and 'I am not the play'. He could have written more about this but time limits what can be put down in an exam. The examiner will be looking for what you do know, not what you don't,

Notice that Thomas' answer responds to the points mentioned under 'Before you begin to write you should think about' (see the question). It is not necessary to write sections addressing these. Thomas refers to them at various appropriate points in his answer.

Using the assessment criteria on page 40, find out how many questions you can answer 'yes' to. All the questions? Thomas would score 22 marks (Level 7+) for Understanding and Response.

WRITTEN EXPRESSION

The writing in this answer is accurate, mature and set out well. It gives the impression of confidence, being structured in an individual, consciously crafted style. This is shown by the following positive features:

*   clearly indicated paragraphs;
*   short quotations from the play, written on separate lines;
*   sentences are varied and all begin with a capital letter and end with a full stop;
*   quotations punctuated just as they are in the play;
*   the correct use of the apostrophe of possession, for example: 'Olivia's capacity for love'.
*   a wide range of punctuation used, i.e. not just commas and full stops;
*   clear communication of ideas by careful use of personal pronouns, i.e. using 'he', 'she' and 'they' instead of full character names when appropriate.

Using the assessment criteria on page 44–5, Thomas' answer would be awarded Level 7+ (16 marks) for Written Expression.

How to mark your Written Expression

Use the assessment criteria opposite. Decide which level best describes your writing following the steps below. Then award yourself the relevant number of marks, according to how well you feel your writing meets the criteria, as described below. Begin with the questions for Level 4.

If you are unable to answer 'yes' to at least two of the questions for Level 4, your written expression is probably at an earlier stage of development and you may be working at Level 3.

Award yourself 5 marks total.

If you are able to answer 'yes' to at least two of the questions for Level 4, go on to consider the questions for Level 5. If you then answer 'yes' to fewer than half the questions for Level 5, you are probably working at Level 4.

Award yourself 6 marks total.

If you are able to answer 'yes' to at least three of the Level 5 questions, you are probably working at Level 5.

Award yourself 9 marks total.

If you are able to answer 'yes' to more than half the questions for Level 5, go on to consider the questions for Level 6. If you then answer 'yes' to fewer than three of the Level 6 questions, you are probably working at Level 5.

Award yourself 9 marks total.

If you are able to answer 'yes' to at least half of the Level 6 questions, then you are probably working at Level 6.

Award yourself 12 marks total.

If you are able to answer 'yes' to at least three of the questions for Level 6, go on to consider the Level 7 questions. If you then answer 'yes' to only one or two questions for Level 7, you are probably working at Level 6.

Award yourself 12 marks total.

If you are able to answer 'yes' to at least three of the questions for Level 7, then you are probably working at Level 7.

Award yourself 15 marks total.

If you are able to answer 'yes' to most of the questions for Level 7, go on to consider the questions for Level 7+. If you then answer 'yes' to fewer than four of the Level 7+ questions, you are probably working at Level 7.

Award yourself 15 marks total.

If you are able to answer 'yes' to all of the questions for Level 7+, you are probably working at a High Level 7 or above.

Award yourself 16 marks total.

SHAKESPEARE ASSESSMENT CRITERIA: WRITTEN EXPRESSION	Yes	No
LEVEL 4 Are ideas generally clearly expressed, i.e. is the meaning clear to the reader?	☐	☐
Is there some use of paragraphs?	☐	☐
Is the punctuation to mark sentences generally accurate, with some punctuation within the sentences?	☐	☐
Is the spelling of simple and common polysyllabic words generally accurate?	☐	☐
Is the handwriting mostly clear and legible?	☐	☐
LEVEL 5 Are ideas clearly expressed and clearly structured, with words usually used precisely and appropriately?	☐	☐
Are simple and complex sentences usually organised into paragraphs?	☐	☐
Is a range of punctuation, including commas, apostrophes and quotation marks, usually used accurately?	☐	☐
Is spelling usually accurate, including words with complex regular patterns?	☐	☐
Is the handwriting generally clear, legible and fluent?	☐	☐
LEVEL 6 Does the writing communicate well, with ideas grouped into paragraphs with a sense of purpose?	☐	☐
Is the vocabulary varied, with a range of appropriate language used in a range of simple and complex sentences?	☐	☐
Is spelling accurate, though there may be errors in difficult words?	☐	☐
Is a range of punctuation usually used correctly to clarify meaning?	☐	☐
Is the handwriting consistently legible and fluent?	☐	☐
LEVEL 7 Is the writing confident, with assured choices of words and style appropriate for the subject?	☐	☐
Are paragraphing and punctuation used correctly?	☐	☐
Is the spelling perfect, except for errors caused by minor slips or through the use of specialised words?	☐	☐
Is the handwriting consistently legible and fluent?	☐	☐
Are grammatical features and vocabulary used accurately, appropriately and effectively?	☐	☐
LEVEL 7+ Is the writing coherent and structured in an individual, consciously crafted style?	☐	☐
Are vocabulary and grammar used to make fine distinctions and/or to emphasise a point of view?	☐	☐
Is the spelling and punctuation almost faultless?	☐	☐
Is the handwriting consistently fluent and legible?	☐	☐

Papers 1 and 2
Determining your level

MARKING GRID

Section	Marks available	Marks scored
Question 1	6	
Question 2	11	
Question 3	11	
Question 4 (a or b)	33	
Total	**61**	

Task 1, 2, or 3	Marks available	Marks scored
Understanding and Response	22	
Written Expression	16	
Total	**38**	

FINDING YOUR LEVEL FOR EACH PAPER

When you have marked a test, enter the marks you scored for each section on the Marking Grid above. Then add them up. Using the total for each test, look at the charts below to determine your level for each test.

Paper 1

Level 3 or below	Level 4	Level 5	Level 6	Level 7 or above
up to 15	16–27	28–38	39–49	50+

Paper 2

Level 3 or below	Level 4	Level 5	Level 6	Level 7 or above
up to 10	11–16	17–23	24–30	31+

FINDING YOUR OVERALL LEVEL IN ENGLISH

After you have worked out separate levels for each paper, add up your total marks. Use this total and the chart below to determine your overall level in English. The chart also shows you how your level in these tests compares with the target level for your age group.

Total for Papers 1 and 2

Level 3 or below	Level 4	Level 5	Level 6	Level 7 or above
up to 26	27–43	44–61	62–79	80+
Working towards target level for age group		Working at target level for age group		Working beyond target level

Grammar section
Spelling, Punctuation and Grammar

Instructions to student

- Before starting to answer questions 1–9 you should spend 10 minutes reading the *Talking in Whispers* and *Robinson Crusoe* extracts on pages 1–2 and 12–13 of the English booklet.

- Spend 1 hour on this section.

- Divide your time as follows:
  - 15 minutes on Part 1 (Sentence Level)
  - 5 minutes on Part 2 (Word Level: Spelling)
  - 8 minutes on Part 3 (Word Level: Parts of Speech)
  - 8 minutes on Part 4 (Word Level: Language Changes)
  - 16 minutes on Part 5 (Text Level)
  - 8 minutes on Part 6 (Word Level: Spelling)

- Write your answers to questions 1–4 and 8–16 on separate paper.

- Check your work carefully.

Grammar section

Start		Finish	

To work on Parts 1–5 of the Grammar section you need the extracts
Talking in Whispers and *The Life and Adventures of Robinson Crusoe*
on pages 1–2 and 12–13 of the English booklet.

Part 1   Sentence Level

Read this sentence from **Robinson Crusoe**:

'When I came down from my appartment in the tree, I look'd about me
again, and the first thing I found was the boat, which lay as the wind and
the sea had toss'd her up upon the land, about two miles on my right
hand.'

*It is a compound sentence. This is to say that it is a series of simple
sentences joined by words called connectives. Connectives are words like,
'although', 'as if', 'when', 'while', 'since', 'after'.*

1

4

Q1

> **List the four connectives used in the sentence above from**
> ***Robinson Crusoe.***

*A simple sentence is a group of words with one verb that makes sense by
itself. It can stand by itself and make sense. For example, 'I came down
from my appartment in the tree.', is a simple sentence.*

2

5

Q2

> **Write out the five simple sentences that have been joined by the**
> **four connectives in the sentence from *Robinson Crusoe*. The first**
> **one has been done for you above.**

Count the number of words in the first sentence of **Talking in Whispers**
*and the number of words in the first sentence, which is the entire first
paragraph, of the* **Robinson Crusoe** *extract.*

First sentence of **Talking in Whispers**.   Number of words [   ]
First sentence of **Robinson Crusoe**. Number of words [   ]

Now read lines 68–70 in **Talking in Whispers**. *This is probably the longest
sentence in this extract, yet in the* **Robinson Crusoe** *extract every
sentence is longer.*

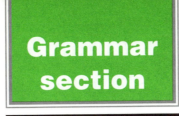

Grammar section

3 | Think of TWO reasons for this difference in sentence length.

A phrase is a group of words (two or more) without a verb. Examples from **Talking in Whispers** *are:*

'with rifle butts'
'An American.'
'the tall one'

Read these words from **Robinson Crusoe**:

'In a word, I had nothing about me but a knife, a tobacco-pipe, and a little tobacco in a box; this was all my provision,... .'

4 | How many of the words are phrases. Why do you think so many have been used?

Part 2   Word Level: Spelling

You will have learnt that language changes over time. One example of this is the way the spelling of some English words has altered. Here are some examples from **Robinson Crusoe**.

5 | Provide the modern spelling of the words in bold type. Use the box after each question for your answer.

a   '**Wrapt** up in the contemplation of my deliverance'.

b   'thick bushy tree like a **firr**'.

Grammar section

Q5c

Q5d

Q5e

Q5f

c 'consider the next day what death I should **dye**'.

d 'by the swelling of the **tyde**'.

e 'when I came down from my **appartment**'.

f 'where I had **hop'd** to find something for my present subsistence'.

Part 3 Word Level: Parts of Speech

*Look at the first paragraph of **Talking in Whispers**.*

'The prisoners who hesitated …'. 'Hesitated' is a verb. The root of this verb is 'hesitate'.

6

> **What part of speech is the word in bold print in each of these sentences?**

Q6a

Q6b

a **Hesitation** always leads to delay.

Part of speech:..

b The cat crept **hesitatingly** into the pipe.

Part of speech:..

c Her **hesitant** answer showed how nervous she was.

Part of speech:...

d **Hesitancy** in striking the ball will lead to a missed penalty.

Part of speech:...

e He who **hesitates** is lost.

Part of speech:...

Part 4   Word Level: Language Changes

You have just seen how spellings have changed. The meaning of words and the order in which they are used has also changed over time.

7

> Here are some examples of language from *Robinson Crusoe* which we are unlikely to use nowadays. Look at the examples below and write each one as it would be written today.

a 'that there should be not one soul sav'd but myself'

....

....

b 'I cast my eyes to the stranded vessel'

....

....

c 'Night coming upon me'

....

....

2

Q7d

2

Q7e

Grammar section

d   'expressively fatigu'd'

....

....

e   'I walk'd as far as I could upon the shore'

....

....

Part 5   Text Level

The way each of the two passages is written adds to the reader's knowledge and understanding of the situation of the two central characters. There are important differences in the way that each extract is written. The situations of Andres in the National Stadium and Robinson Crusoe on the shore have a different sense of time and a different sense of urgency. This is shown in the organisation of the sentences and paragraphs.

*In **Talking in Whispers** time is very short for Andres. Events happen quickly and each one increases Andres' involvement and danger.*

*In **Robinson Crusoe** time is not short. He may not be entirely safe but all immediate danger is past. He is at least out of the sea and on the shore. If he is to continue to survive he must notice every detail of his new surroundings. The writer also wants the reader to be able to imagine being in that situation.*

NOTE

'Contrast' in a question means that you have to point out the differences between things.

> **Examiner's tip**
>
> To answer Question 8 you need to find examples of how slowly the story of Robinson Crusoe develops and how quickly the story about Andres moves. Contrast the amount and kind of detail in both extracts. Contrast the length and number of paragraphs. For example, there is an astonishing example of a one-phrase paragraph in **Talking in Whispers**. (Look at the first half of **Talking in Whispers**.)

8

> **Contrast the way the writers describe the situations of Andres in the National Stadium and Robinson Crusoe on the shore.**

A paragraph from the *Robinson Crusoe* extract often consists of a long complex sentence. For example see lines 39-46. Such a sentence usually only ever appears in writing. It would sound very strange if anybody spoke like this.

On the other hand, in *Talking in Whispers*, it is easy to imagine people speaking some of the paragraphs. The writer has tried to give the impression of speech. It is not actual speech but the writer knows enough of what spontaneous speech sounds like to be able to imitate it for his story.

9

> **Think about what you know about real speech. Contrast the imitation of it in *Talking in Whispers* with the language and grammar of *Robinson Crusoe*.**

Part 6 Word Level: Spelling

These questions assess your ability to explain spelling patterns, show understanding of word formation and spell correctly.

Read this passage about diet in hospitals.

All hospital dieticians agree that correct diet is of great <u>importance</u> in making treatment a <u>success</u>. It is a physiological <u>necessity</u> and has important <u>psychological</u> benefits. Careful consideration of the <u>quality</u> and quantity of food and drink will help on the road to <u>complete</u> recovery <u>whether</u> fighting disease or recovering from surgery.

Now look at the underlined words and answer the questions which follow.

10 *Look at the noun 'importance'.*

> **Write the adjective formed from the same stem.**

Grammar section

11 *Look at the words 'necessity' and 'quality'.*

a Write down the plural of one of these words.

b Explain what spelling pattern the formation of this plural follows.

12 *Look at the word 'psychological'. This word begins with the prefix, 'psycho-'.*

Explain what the prefix 'psycho-' means. Then write down another word (but not 'psychology') which begins with the prefix 'psycho-' or 'psych-'.

13 *Look at the noun 'success'.*

a Write down the plural of 'success'.

b Write down an adjective formed from 'success'.

14 *Look at the verb 'complete'.*

Write down a noun formed from the same stem.

15 *Look at the word 'whether'.*

Write down a common homophone (a word which sounds the same but is spelled differently) for this word and use it correctly in a sentence.

16 Write down another pair of homophones and explain what each word in the pair means. You can base this pair on a word from the passage or choose other words.

Part 1   Sentence Level

1   The four connectives are:

- When
- and
- which
- about

One mark for each correct answer: 4 marks
Total 4 marks

2   The five simple sentences are:

- I came down from my appartment in the tree.
- I look'd about me again.
- The first thing I found was the boat.
- The boat lay as the wind and sea had tossed her up upon the land.
- The boat was about two miles on my right hand.

One mark for each correct answer: 5 marks
Total 5 marks

3   Possible reasons are:

- 18th century writers wrote much longer sentences than writers usually do today.
- Robinson Crusoe has more time to explore his surroundings than Andres has in ***Talking in Whispers***.
- James Watson uses shorter sentences in ***Talking in Whispers*** to create a sense of danger and urgency.
- The writer of Robinson Crusoe wants his reader to be able to imagine Crusoe's situation and so includes lots of detail.

Two marks each for any two of the above reasons: 4 marks
Total 4 marks

4   There are **seven** phrases in this extract:

- In a word
- about me
- but a knife
- a tobacco-pipe
- a little tobacco
- in a box
- all my provision

Award one mark for each phrase identified up to a total of six: 6 marks
Total 6 marks

Part 2 Word Level: Spelling

5 Here are the modern spellings of the words in bold type.
a wrapped
b fir
c die
d tide
e apartment
f hoped

Award one mark for each correct spelling: 6 marks
Total 6 marks

Part 3 Word Level: Parts of Speech

6 These are the correctly identified parts of speech:
a noun
b adverb
c adjective
d noun
e verb

Award two marks for each correct answer: 10 marks
Total 10 marks

Part 4 Word Level: Language Changes

7 Here you have been asked to rewrite the language examples from **Robinson Crusoe** as they might be written today. If your answers are similar to the ones below then award yourself the marks.
a 'I was the only one saved' *or*
'I was the only survivor'
b 'I looked at the stranded ship' *or*
'I glanced at the ship' *or*
'I looked towards the ship'
c 'Night was falling' *or*
'It was nearly night' *or*
'It was going dark'
d 'tired out' *or*
'I was very tired' *or*
'exhausted'
e 'I walked as far as I could along the shore'

Award two marks for each answer: 10 marks
Total 10 marks

Part 5   Text Level

There are two questions in this section and each is worth 10 marks.

8   This question expects you to point out some of the differences in the way the two extracts are written. If you have five contrasts that are similar to the ones that follow then give yourself two marks for each. Remember any **five** of the following differences will give you the full 10 marks for this question.

- There are six paragraphs in the ***Robinson Crusoe*** extract and more than thirty in ***Talking in Whispers***. Short paragraphs give a sense of urgency and danger. Long paragraphs give the impression of time moving slowly.

- Lots of dangerous things happen suddenly in ***Talking in Whispers***. So there are lots of short sentences and even one-word paragraphs. There are very few events in the ***Robinson Crusoe*** extract although there is plenty of detail about what he thought and noticed. His thoughts are complicated and detailed and so are the sentences that tell the reader what he is thinking. Sometimes one long sentence makes one long paragraph.

- Phrases in ***Robinson Crusoe*** are used for lists. Phrases in ***Talking in Whispers*** are used to hurry the action forward and to introduce extra excitement. For example, 'An American.' in line 17.

- The language in ***Robinson Crusoe*** is difficult. The language in ***Talking in Whispers*** is simpler. For example, 'After I had solac'd my mind with the comfortable part of my condition,' from ***Robinson Crusoe*** compared with, 'Andres felt a thrill of hope.' from ***Talking in Whispers.*** Both sentences refer to hope but one sentence is much simpler. The difference is caused by the way writing styles have changed over time.

- Robinson Crusoe is by himself. Andres is part of a packed crowd. He can only notice bits and pieces of what happens. Robinson Crusoe, however, is entirely alone in this extract and can leisurely notice as much as he wants to. The language structures of the two passages reinforce this difference in their two situations.

Award two marks for each similar contrast: 10 marks

Total 10 marks

9   What are the features of spontaneous or 'real' speech? Which of these features does the ***Talking in Whispers*** extract imitate? Why do you think no one speaks (although they may write) in the style of the ***Robinson Crusoe*** extract?

If your answer contains five similar points to the ones below, award yourself the full 10 marks.

- There are incomplete sentences in ***Talking in Whispers***. For example, 'But –'. This is an incomplete and interrupted sentence. This is a feature of real speech.

- 'Permiso! Give us passage, folks – it's for a good cause.' Informal expressions and sudden changes of subject are also features of real speech.

- Short sentences that rely on the person being present to make proper sense. For example, in ***Talking in Whispers***, 'That's my friend – the tall one.' A real speaker could point if there was any doubt which person was being referred to. A writer has to use description. Here there is a bit of both because it is an imitation of real speech.

- Repetition as in 'Please – please let me through...' is a feature of real speech in ***Talking in Whispers***.

Robinson Crusoe has **no** features of real or spontaneous speech. There are plenty of structures that are usually only found in writing. Some of these are:

- Long complex sentences with subordinate clauses.

- Long compound sentences using three or four connectives with words missed but understood. See the example that was used in question 2 in the Sentence Level Section on page 48. You had to write out the five simple sentences that made up one sentence; for two of your simple sentences you had to add the words 'the boat' that were understood in the original, long sentence.

- Long complicated single sentence paragraphs that can be re-read if necessary. It is impossible to do this in real speech so people do not speak in this style.

Award two marks for each similar contrast: 10 marks
Total 10 marks

Part 6   Word Level: Spellings

10   important
1 mark
Total 1 mark

11a   equalities *or* necessities
1 mark
   b   When 'y' follows a consonant, change the 'y' to 'i' before adding the plural ending '-es'.
1 mark
Total 2 marks

12a   Answer should include 'psycho' means 'mind' or a similar explanation.
1 mark
   b   There are many appropriate words, e.g. psychiatry/psychopath, psychedelic, etc. (Check spelling and other alternatives in a dictionary.)
1 mark
Total 2 marks

13a   successes
1 mark

   b   successful
   (Note: 'successive' is not formed from 'success'.)
1 mark
Total 2 marks

14   completion *or* completeness *or* completedness
1 mark
Total 1 mark

15   The word 'weather' and a sentence or phrase which shows understanding of the its meaning.
1 mark
Total 1 mark

16   An example from the passage is the word 'road' (rode). You could use any other pair of homophones with an accurate explanation of their meanings. (Check spellings and meanings in a dictionary).
1 mark
Total 1 mark

Grammar section
Determining your level

MARKING GRID

GRAMMAR SECTION *Pages 48–54*

		Marks available	Marks scored
Part 1	Sentence Level	19	
Part 2	Word Level: Spelling	6	
Part 3	Word Level: Parts of Speech	10	
Part 4	Word Level: Language Changes	10	
Part 5	Text Level	20	
Part 6	Word Level: Spelling	10	
Total		**75**	

FINDING YOUR LEVEL

When you have marked this section, enter the marks you scored for each part on the Marking Grid above. Then add them up. Using your total score, look at the charts below to determine your level.

Level 4 or below	Level 5	Level 6	Level 7	Above Level 7
1–15	16–30	31–45	46–60	61–75

Talking in Whispers

This is part of a novel by James Watson. It is set in Chile in the 1970s during the rule of General Pinochet and his army. Political prisoners are being taken by the army* to the National Stadium. Andres, a teenage boy, is searching for his friend, Braulio.

Andres stayed clear of the crowd. He watched the arrival of another truck. The soldiers did not care if their brutality was witnessed by hundreds of people. Those prisoners who hesitated as they climbed from the truck were hastened on their way with rifle butts.

'Move, scum!'   5

Suddenly Andres broke forward, seeking a gap in the wall of people. 'Braulio!' There was no doubt. His friend had jumped from the truck. He was handcuffed. 'Braulio!' Andres fought to get through the crowd.

Braulio Altuna stood a head taller than the other prisoners in line. A stream of blood had congealed down one side of his face.   10

Andres forgot his own danger. He must get to Braulio, at the very least let him know that somebody had proof that he was alive.

'Please – please let me through – my friend is out there!' Andres looked to be having no luck in prising a way through the crowd when he spotted a tall man in a white mack, making better progress.   15

'Permiso! Give us a passage, folks – it's for a good cause.'

An American.

Andres tucked himself in behind the man, burly, fair-haired, with out-thrust arm, shoving a sideways path towards the truck and the gates of the stadium.   20

Andres got so close to the American that he could have picked his pocket. He glanced down and saw that the man was holding something behind him, wrapped in a carrier bag.

For an instant, Andres decided that the American had a gun. Yet the compulsion to make contact with Braulio proved greater than Andres' fear that   25
he might have landed himself in a shoot-out.

The object which the American slipped from the carrier bag had indeed many more shots than a pistol. A camera! He's a pressman. Andres felt a thrill of hope. Here comes the American cavalry! He was right behind the pressman. He shouted in Spanish: 30

'Give him room!' And then in a low voice only audible to the American, 'The world's got to know what's happening here.'

'You bet it has.' The pressman took Andres in in one friendly – even grateful – glance. They were comrades. Together they breasted a way through the crowd.   35

'That's my friend – the tall one.'

The last prisoners were being driven from the truck. One was not fast enough to please his guards. He was hurt, hobbling, gripping his side in pain.

'Step on it, you red scab!'

The American's camera was in the air. A rifle butt swung against the   40
stumbling prisoner.

Click-whirr, click-whirr – the scene was banked, recorded.

Braulio had turned, stepping out of line. He protested at the guard's action and immediately drew soldiers round him like wasps to honey.

Click-whirr, click-whirr. The toppling of Braulio was captured. Here was   45
evidence for the time when villainy would be brought to justice.

* The 'Black Berets'

Yet here also was terrible danger. The American photographer had himself been snapped by the eye of the officer commanding the troops. 'Christ. They've spotted me!' He lowered his camera swiftly below the shoulders of the crowd. He shifted, half-face towards Andres. He seemed paralysed by fear.   50

The American pushed the camera into Andres' hand. 'Take this – I'm finished.'

'But –'

'I beg you. The film in that camera…'

The officer and his men were clubbing a passage through the crowd   55
towards the American. Andres ducked the camera through the open zip of his jacket. 'Who shall I say?' He was being carried away from the pressman by the retreat of the crowd.

'Chailey – Don Chailey!' He yelled the name of his newspaper too but the words did not carry to Andres who found himself squeezed step by step away   60
from the oncoming troops.

The crowd had saved Andres. It had no power to delay sentence upon the American. The soldiers were all round him. Momentarily his fair hair could be seen between their helmets. Then his arms went up above his head. He folded under a rampage of blows. He was hammered to the ground. He was   65
kicked in the body, in the head, his hands stamped upon, his ribs skewered with iron-shod boots.

And now they were searching for his camera. They were demanding answers from the crowd, accusing them, turning their violence upon the innocent, frisking everyone who could have been within orbit of the American.   70

For an eternal second, Andres stood and watched. He saw Don Chailey dragged towards the stadium entrance. He saw him flung into one of the turnstiles.

Andres trembled as if touched by an electrified fence. Till now, he had wandered helplessly, insignificant. Soaked to the skin, he had arrived at the   75
final blank wall and closed gate. His brain, his heart, his passionate resolve – they were nothing in the face of the Junta's untouchable strength.

But now… A chance in a million, an encounter lasting no longer than two minutes, had changed everything. He was in possession of something the military would like to get their hands on – proof of their brutality. What's more,   80
Andres was witness to what the Black Berets had done to a citizen of the United States of America.

The Americans don't pour millions of dollars into Chile for us to beat up their newspapermen. Andres was at the street corner, poised for flight. All at once he had a purpose, a direction, a next step. He tapped the camera   85
reverently. Somehow I must contact the Resistance. What's in this camera might be just as valuable as bullets.

Would you be put in prison if you complained about your school?

YOUTH ACTION

HOW YOU CAN HELP

Amnesty International is a worldwide human rights movement independent of any government, political or religious ideology. Amnesty campaigns through its membership by the simple technique of **letter writing.** Members write short and respectful letters to the heads of governments, justice ministers or whoever Amnesty thinks is the appropriate person in authority. The letter requests the immediate and unconditional release of a prisoner of conscience, an end to torture or a halt to an execution.

JOIN AMNESTY

You can join the one million plus members of Amnesty working in over 150 countries.

● Your **school, college or youth club** could affiliate to Amnesty and join over 450 youth groups campaigning through Amnesty throughout the UK.

● Affiliation costs **£21.00** a year, and your group will then receive regular mailings about Amnesty's campaigns and concerns around the world.

SPREAD THE WORD

Groups play an important role in informing those around them.

● Why not do an assembly on Amnesty or hire a video to promote human rights as an issue?

● **Send NOW for more information**

PLEASE SEND ME

NO. OF COPIES

New Release Youth magazine @ **75p each (YA096)**

[ ] [ ]

Youth Action Start-Up Pack @ **£1.50 each (YA386)**

[ ] [ ] [ ]

Letter writing tips **Free (YS390)**

Video list **Free (OM130)**

Assembly Pack **Free (YA381)**

More copies of this leaflet **Free** (tick amount) [10] [20] [30]

Membership form

● I wish to become an **individual member** of Amnesty International and enclose a cheque/postal order for **£21** (**£7.50 students and under 22, Senior Citizens and claimants**)

Name .... Age ....

Address ....

....

Postcode .... Tel ....

Affiliation form

● My **group/organisation** hereby applies for affiliation to Amnesty International and we enclose a cheque for £ ....

Rates of affiliation (please tick box as appropriate)

[ ] £21 pa up to 100 members

[ ] £27 pa 101 – 2,000 members

[ ] £32 pa 2,001 – 5,000 members

[ ] £45 pa 5,001 – 10,000 members
    (minimum for regional organisations)

[ ] £64 pa 10,001 – 20,000 members
    (minimum for national organisations)

Contact name ....

Name of organisation ....

Address ....

Postcode .... Tel ....

Email address ....

Please write to: Amnesty International United Kingdom, **99-119 Rosebery Avenue, London EC1R 4RE** Tel: 0171-814 6200

http://www.amnesty.org.uk/

YA382

Should you be executed if you kill someone? Mohammad was.

Mohammed Aelim, aged 17, was hanged in Dhaka Jail in Bangladesh

● AN END TO THE DEATH PENALTY

Amnesty International opposes the death penalty in all circumstances and in all countries. And considers it to be the most inhuman punishment possible. The death penalty does nothing to prevent violent crime and is a violation of the right to life.

The death penalty is cruel and unjust, irrevocable and immoral. There have been many established cases of conviction of innocent persons. Everyone knows that the law can make mistakes but you cannot release the innocent after death.

Over 86 countries have ceased to use the death penalty and Amnesty International is campaigning to persuade the remaining 94 governments to stop executing their own citizens.

STOP PRESS

Six months after Amnesty's involvement in Nafije's case her freedom has been secured. Her friends remain in custody. Amnesty International needs your help to continue its work.
Turn over to find out what you can do to help

YOUTH ACTION

Nafije was.

For forming a 'Freedom Society' in protest against a decision to withdraw Albanian language lessons at her school. She was arrested and tried along with three friends. According to evidence produced in court Nafije had done well in school and did not have any record of anti-social behaviour. She was sentenced to 4 years in prison. This is the sort of injustice Amnesty International is fighting against.

● STRIVING TO ABOLISH TORTURE

Despite a universal ban on torture proclaimed by the United Nations, the practice — ordered or condoned by governments — still takes place in one out of three countries.

Torture can take many forms. Electric shocks, sexual assaults, severe beatings and submerging in water or excrement are common. Psychological torture ranges from mock executions and threats to loved ones, to deprivation of food and sleep, or of hearing, seeing or feeling.

Amnesty International rejects the use of torture in all circumstances. It has drawn up a 12-point programme to prevent tortureand is seeking to have this adopted by all countries. Amnesty also works to help individual victims. Your support is needed to help stamp out this terrible violation of human rights.

● CAMPAIGNING FOR THE RELEASE OF PRISONERS OF CONSCIENCE

Hundreds, if not thousands, of people all over the world are prisoners of conscience — men, women and children imprisoned for their peacefully-held political or religious views, their ethnic origins, or because of the language they speak.

Amnesty International campaigns for the immediate and unconditional release of prisoners of conscience held in over 70 countries. Amnesty International believes that all prisoners should be given a prompt and fair trial, and that no prisoner should be tortured, ill-treated or put to death.

Would you be tortured because of your parents' views? Ali was.

Ali Hama Salih was 12 years old when arrested and interrogated in Iraq. A few days later his body was returned to his family showing marks of torture

4

Romeo and Juliet
Act 1 Scene 5, Lines 39–125
Scene 5 Verona   A hall in Capulet's house

ROMEO	[*To a Servingman*] What lady's that which doth enrich the hand	
		40
	Of yonder knight?	
SERVINGMAN	I know not, sir.	
ROMEO	O she doth teach the torches to burn bright!	
	It seems she hangs upon the cheek of night	
	As a rich jewel in an Ethiop's ear –	45
	Beauty too rich for use, for earth too dear:	
	So shows a snowy dove trooping with crows,	
	As yonder lady o'er her fellows shows.	
	The measure done, I'll watch her place of stand,	
	And touching hers, make blessed my rude hand.	50
	Did my heart love till now? forswear it, sight!	
	For I ne'er saw true beauty till this night.	
TYBALT	This, by his voice, should be a Montague.	
	Fetch me my rapier, boy.	

[*Exit Page*]

	What dares the slave.	
	Come hither, covered with an antic face,	55
	To fleer and scorn at our solemnity?	
	Now by the stock and honour of my kin,	
	To strike him dead I hold it not a sin.	
CAPULET	Why, how now, kinsman, wherefore storm you so?	
TYBALT	Uncle, this is a Montague, our foe:	60
	A villain, that is hither come in spite,	
	To scorn at our solemnity this night.	
CAPULET	Young Romeo is it?	
TYBALT	'Tis he, that villain Romeo.	
CAPULET	Content thee, gentle coz, let him alone,	
	'A bears him like a portly gentleman;	65
	And to say truth, Verona brags of him	
	To be a virtuous and well-governed youth.	
	I would not for the wealth of all this town	
	Here in my house do him disparagement;	
	Therefore be patient, take no note of him;	70
	It is my will, the which if thou respect,	
	Show a fair presence, and put off these frowns,	
	An ill-beseeming semblance for a feast.	
TYBALT	It fits when such a villain is a guest:	
	I'll not endure him.	
CAPULET	He shall be endured.	75
	What, goodman boy, I say he shall, go to!	
	Am I the master here, or you? go to!	
	You'll not endure him? God shall mend my soul,	
	You'll make a mutiny among my guests!	
	You will set cock-a-hoop! you'll be the man!	80

TYBALT	Why, uncle, 'tis a shame.
CAPULET	Go to, go to,
	You are a saucy boy. Is't so indeed?
	This trick may chance to scathe you, I know what.
	You must contrary me! Marry, 'tis time. –
	Well said, my hearts! – You are a princox, go,
	Be quiet, or – More light, more light! – For shame,
	I'll make you quiet, what! – Cheerly, my hearts!
TYBALT	Patience perforce with wilful choler meeting
	Makes my flesh tremble in their difference greeting:
	I will withdraw, but this intrusion shall,
	Now seeming sweet, convert to bitt'rest gall. *Exit*
ROMEO	[*To Juliet*] If I profane with my unworthiest hand
	This holy shrine, the gentle sin is this,
	My lips, two blushing pilgrims, ready stand
	To smooth that rough touch with a tender kiss.
JULIET	Good pilgrim, you do wrong your hand too much,
	Which mannerly devotion shows in this,
	For saints have hands that pilgrims' hands do touch,
	And palm to palm is holy palmers' kiss.
ROMEO	Have not saints lips, and holy palmers too?
JULIET	Ay, pilgrim, lips that they must use in prayer.
ROMEO	O then, dear saint, let lips do what hands do:
	They pray, grant thou, lest faith turn to despair.
JULIET	Saints do not move, though grant for prayers' sake.
ROMEO	Then move not while my prayer's effect I take.
	Thus from my lips, by thine, my sin is purged.
	[*Kissing her.*]
JULIET	Then have my lips the sin that they have took.
ROMEO	Sin from my lips? O trespass sweetly urged!
	Give me my sin again.
	[*Kissing her again.*]
JULIET	You kiss by th'book.
NURSE	Madam, your mother craves a word with you.
ROMEO	What is her mother?
NURSE	Marry, bachelor.
	Her mother is the lady of the house,
	And a good lady, and a wise and virtuous.
	I nursed her daughter that you talked withal;
	I tell you, he that can lay hold of her
	Shall have the chinks.
ROMEO	Is she a Capulet?
	O dear account! my life is my foe's debt.
BENVOLIO	Away, be gone, the sport is at the best.
ROMEO	Ay, so I fear, the more is my unrest.
CAPULET	Nay, gentlemen, prepare not to be gone,
	We have a trifling foolish banquet towards.
	[*They whisper in his ear.*]
	Is it e'en so? Why then I thank you all.
	I thank you, honest gentlemen, good night.
	More torches here, come on! then let's go to bed.
	Ah, sirrah, by my fay, it waxes late,
	I'll to my rest.

Line numbers: 85, 90, 95, 100, 105, 110, 115, 120, 125

Macbeth
Act 1 Scene 7
Macbeth's castle   Near the Great Hall

Hautboys. Torches. Enter a butler and many servants with dishes and
service over the stage. Then enter MACBETH.

MACBETH	If it were done when 'tis done, then 'twere well	
	It were done quickly. If th'assassination	
	Could trammel up the consequence and catch	
	With his surcease, success, that but this blow	
	Might be the be-all and the end-all – here,	5
	But here, upon this bank and shoal of time,	
	We'd jump the life to come. But in these cases,	
	We still have judgement here that we but teach	
	Bloody instructions, which being taught, return	
	To plague th'inventor. This even-handed justice	10
	Commends th'ingredience of our poisoned chalice	
	To our own lips. He's here in double trust:	
	First, as I am his kinsman and his subject,	
	Strong both against the deed; then, as his host,	
	Who should against his murderer shut the door,	15
	Not bear the knife myself. Besides, this Duncan	
	Hath borne his faculties so meek, hath been	
	So clear in his great office, that his virtues	
	Will plead like angels, trumpet-tongued against	
	The deep damnation of his taking-off.	20
	And pity, like a naked newborn babe	
	Striding the blast, or heaven's cherubin horsed	
	Upon the sightless couriers of the air,	
	Shall blow the horrid deed in every eye,	
	That tears shall drown the wind. I have no spur	25
	To prick the sides of my intent, but only	
	Vaulting ambition which o'erleaps itself	
	And falls on th'other –	

Enter LADY [MACBETH]

How now? What news?

LADY MACBETH	He has almost supped. Why have you left the	
	chamber?	
MACBETH	Hath he asked for me?	
LADY MACBETH	Know you not he has?	30
MACBETH	We will proceed no further in this business.	
	He hath honoured me of late, and I have bought	
	Golden opinions from all sorts of people,	
	Which would be worn now in their newest gloss,	
	Not cast aside so soon.	
LADY MACBETH	Was the hope drunk	35
	Wherein you dressed yourself? Hath it slept since?	
	And wakes it now to look so green and pale	
	At what it did so freely? From this time,	

Such I account thy love. Art thou afeard
To be the same in thine own act and valour, 40
As thou art in desire? Wouldst thou have that
Which thou esteem'st the ornament of life,
And live a coward in thine own esteem,
Letting I dare not wait upon I would,
Like the poor cat i'th'adage?

MACBETH   Prithee, peace. 45
I dare do all that may become a man;
Who dares do more is none.

LADY MACBETH   What beast was't then
That made you break this enterprise to me?
When you durst do it, then you were a man.
And to be more than what you were, you would 50
Be so much more the man. Nor time, nor place
Did then adhere, and yet you would make both.
They have made themselves and their fitness now
Does unmake you. I have given suck and know
How tender 'tis to love the babe that milks me: 55
I would, while it was smiling in my face,
Have plucked my nipple from his boneless gums
And dashed the brains out, had I so sworn
As you have done to this.

MACBETH   If we should fail?

LADY MACBETH   We fail?
But screw your courage to the sticking place, 60
And we'll not fail. When Duncan is asleep,
Whereto the rather shall his day's hard journey
Soundly invite him, his two chamberlains
Will I with wine and wassail so convince
That memory, the warder of the brain, 65
Shall be a fume, and the receipt of reason
A limbeck only. When in swinish sleep
Their drenched natures lies as in a death,
What cannot you and I perform upon
Th'unguarded Duncan? What not put upon 70
His spongy officers, who shall bear the guilt
Of our great quell?

MACBETH   Bring forth men-children only,
For thy undaunted mettle should compose
Nothing but males. Will it not be received,
When we have marked with blood those sleepy two 75
Of his own chamber and used their very daggers,
That they have done't?

LADY MACBETH   Who dares receive it other,
As we shall make our griefs and clamour roar
Upon his death?

MACBETH   I am settled and bend up
Each corporal agent to this terrible feat. 80
Away, and mock the time with fairest show,
False face must hide what the false heart doth know.
                                                    Exeunt

Twelfth Night
Act 1 Scene 5, Lines 136–253
Scene 5   A room in Olivia's house

OLIVIA	Give me my veil; come throw it o'er my face. We'll once more hear Orsino's embassy.	

Enter VIOLA

VIOLA	The honourable lady of the house, which is she?	
OLIVIA	Speak to me; I shall answer for her. Your will?	140
VIOLA	Most radiant, exquisite, and unmatchable beauty – I pray you tell me if this be the lady of the house, for I never saw her. I would be loath to cast away my speech: for besides that it is excellently well penned, I have taken great pains to con it. Good beauties, let me sustain no scorn; I am very comptible, even to the least sinister usage.	145
OLIVIA	Whence came you, sir?	
VIOLA	I can say little more than I have studied, and that question's out of my part. Good gentle one, give me modest assurance if you be the lady of the house, that I may proceed in my speech.	150
OLIVIA	Are you a comedian?	
VIOLA	No, my profound heart; and yet, by the very fangs of malice, I swear, I am not that I play. Are you the lady of the house?	
OLIVIA	If I do not usurp myself, I am.	
VIOLA	Most certain, if you are she, you do usurp yourself: for what is yours to bestow is not yours to reserve. But this is from my commission. I will on with my speech in your praise, and then show you the heart of my message.	155
OLIVIA	Come to what is important in't: I forgive you the praise.	
VIOLA	Alas, I took great pains to study it, and 'tis poetical.	160
OLIVIA	It is the more like to be feigned; I pray you keep it in. I heard you were saucy at my gates, and allowed your approach rather to wonder at you than to hear you. If you be not mad, be gone; if you have reason, be brief. 'Tis not that time of moon with me to make one in so skipping a dialogue.	165
MARIA	Will you hoist sail, sir? Here lies your way.	
VIOLA	No, good swabber, I am to hull here a little longer. Some mollification for your giant, sweet lady! Tell me your mind, I am a messenger.	
OLIVIA	Sure you have some hideous matter to deliver, when the courtesy of it is so fearful. Speak your office.	170
VIOLA	It alone concerns your ear. I bring no overture of war, no taxation of homage; I hold the olive in my hand; my words are as full of peace as matter.	
OLIVIA	Yet you began rudely. What are you? What would you?	175
VIOLA	The rudeness that hath appeared in me I learned from my entertainment. What I am, and what I would, are as secret as maidenhead: to your ears, divinity; to any other's profanation.	
OLIVIA	Give us the place alone; we will hear this divinity.	

[*Exeunt Maria and Attendants*]

	Now, sir, what is your text?	180
VIOLA	Most sweet lady –	
OLIVIA	A comfortable doctrine, and much may be said of it. Where lies your text?	
VIOLA	In Orsino's bosom.	
OLIVIA	In his bosom? In what chapter of his bosom?	185
VIOLA	To answer by the method, in the first of his heart.	
OLIVIA	O I have read it. It is heresy. Have you no more to say?	
VIOLA	Good madam, let me see your face.	
OLIVIA	Have you any commission from your lord to negotiate with my face? You are now out of your text, but we will draw the curtain and show you the picture. [*Unveiling*] Look you, sir, such a one I was this present. Is't not well done?	190
VIOLA	Excellently done, if God did all.	
OLIVIA	'Tis in grain, sir; 'twill endure wind and weather.	
VIOLA	'Tis beauty truly blent, whose red and white Nature's own sweet and cunning hand laid on. Lady, you are the cruell'st she alive, If you will lead these graces to the grave, And leave the world no copy.	195
OLIVIA	O sir, I will not be so hard-hearted: I will give out divers schedules of my beauty. It shall be inventoried and every particle and utensil labelled to my will, as, *item*, two lips, indifferent red; *item*, two grey eyes, with lids to them; *item*, one neck, one chin, and so forth. Were you sent hither to 'praise me?	200
VIOLA	I see you what you are. You are too proud; But if you were the devil, you are fair! My lord and master loves you. O such love Could be but recompensed, though you were crowned The nonpareil of beauty.	205
OLIVIA	How does he love me?	
VIOLA	With adorations, fertile tears, With groans that thunder love, with sighs of fire.	210
OLIVIA	Your lord does know my mind. I cannot love him. Yet I suppose him virtuous, know him noble, Of great estate, of fresh and stainless youth; In voices well divulged, free, learned, and valiant, And in dimension, and the shape of nature, A gracious person. But yet I cannot love him. He might have took his answer long ago.	215
VIOLA	If I did love you in my master's flame, With such a suff'ring, such a deadly life, In your denial I would find no sense; I would not understand it.	220
OLIVIA	Why, what would you?	
VIOLA	Make me a willow cabin at your gate, And call upon my soul within the house; Write loyal cantons of contemned love, And sing them loud even in the dead of night; Hallow your name to the reverberate hills, And make the babbling gossip of the air Cry out 'Olivia!' O you should not rest Between the elements of air and earth	225 230

10

	But you should pity me!	
OLIVIA	You might do much.	
	What is your parentage?	
VIOLA	Above my fortunes, yet my state is well:	
	I am a gentleman.	
OLIVIA	Get you to your lord.	
	I cannot love him, Let him send no more –	235
	Unless (perchance) you come to me again,	
	To tell me how he takes it. Fare you well.	
	I thank you for your pains. Spend this for me.	
VIOLA	I am no fee'd post, lady; keep your purse;	
	My master, not myself, lacks recompense.	240
	Love makes his heart of flint that you shall love,	
	And let your fervour like my master's be	
	Placed in contempt. Farewell, fair cruelty. *Exit*	
OLIVIA	'What is your parentage?'	
	'Above my fortunes, yet my state is well:	245
	I am a gentleman.' I'll be sworn thou art;	
	Thy tongue, thy face, thy limbs, actions, and spirit	
	Do give thee five-fold blazon. Not too fast! Soft, soft!	
	Unless the master were the man – How now?	
	Even so quickly may one catch the plague?	250
	Methinks I feel this youth's perfections	
	With an invisible and subtle stealth	
	To creep in at mine eyes. Well, let it be.	

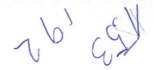

Robinson Crusoe

This is part of the story by Daniel Defoe about a shipwrecked sailor. It was first published in 1719. Robinson Crusoe is the only survivor and has struggled to the shore.

I walk'd about on the shore, lifting up my hands, and my whole being, as may say, wrapt up in the contemplation of my deliverance, making a thousand gestures and motions which I cannot describe, reflecting upon all my comrades that were drown'd, and that there should not be one soul sav'd but my self; for, as for them, I never saw them afterwards, or any sign of them, except three of their hats, one cap, and two shoes that were not fellows.

I cast my eyes to the stranded vessel, when the breach and froth of the sea being so big, I could hardly see it, it lay so far off, and considered Lord! how was it possible I could get on shore?

After I had solac'd my mind with the comfortable part of my condition, I began to look round me to see what kind of place I was in, and what was next to be done, and I soon found my comforts abate, and that in a word I had a dreadful deliverance: for I was wet, had no clothes to shift me, nor any thing either to eat or drink to comfort me, neither did I see any prospect before me, but that of perishing with hunger, or being devour'd by wild beasts; and that which was particularly afflicting to me was that I had no weapon either to hunt and kill any creature for my sustenance, or to defend my self against any other creature that might desire to kill me for theirs. In a word, I had nothing about me but a knife, a tobacco-pipe, and a little tobacco in a box; this was all my provision, and this threw me into terrible agonies of mind, that for a while I ran about like a mad-man. Night coming upon me, I began with a heavy heart to consider what would be my lot if there were any ravenous beasts in that country, seeing at night they always come abroad for their prey.

All the remedy that offer'd to my thoughts at that time was to get up into a thick bushy tree like a firr, but thorny, which grew near me, and where I resolv'd to sit all night, and consider the next day what death I should dye, for as yet I saw no prospect of life; I walk'd about a furlong from the shore, to see if I could find any fresh water to drink, which I did, to my great joy; and having drunk and put a little tobacco in my mouth to prevent hunger, I went to the tree, and getting up into it, endeavour'd to place my self so, as that if I should sleep I might not fall; and having cut me a short stick, like a truncheon, for my defence, I took up my lodging, and having been excessively fatigu'd, I fell fast asleep and slept as comfortably as, I believe, few could have done in my condition, and found my self the most refresh'd with it that I think I ever was on such an occasion.

1

5

10

15

20

25

30

35

When I wak'd it was broad day, the weather clear, and the storm abated, so that the sea did not rage and swell as before: but that which surpris'd me most was that the ship was lifted off in the night from the sand where she lay, by the swelling of the tyde, and was driven up almost as far as the rock which I first mention'd, where I had been so bruis'd by the dashing me against it; this being within about a mile from the shore where I was, and the ship seeming to stand upright still, I wish'd my self on board, that, at least, I might save some necessary things for my use. When I came down from my appartment in the tree, I look'd about me again, and the first thing I found was the boat, which lay as the wind and the sea had toss'd her up upon the land, about two miles on my right hand. I walk'd as far as I could upon the shore to have got to her, but found a neck or inlet of water between me and the boat, which was about half a mile broad, so I came back for the present, being more intent upon getting at the ship, where I hop'd to find something for my present subsistence.

40

45

50

54